Navigators of the Contemporary

<u>BDs change</u> - have 'conversations' w/ villagers
about how village life + BDs is it has
+ is changing. Not interviews, as much as
conversations. Not sure I understand the
difference

<u>Intro Fw book</u> - we were trained in and did
much traditional ethnography +but
like the discipline we have <u>changed</u>
Our field projects + experiences in
this book, from Inuh Tp in 1971 to
Tsm guide, represent / shed light
on / are a lens thru which the evolution /
changes in anthro can be viewed
        Also we hope this book offers anthro
students an understanding of + exposes
them to, even it only sketchily, a r n
a range of cultures - Inuh Tp, BDs village,
Eng G's, TAs to Amer. bb players.

Navigators of the Contemporary

Why Ethnography Matters

DAVID A. WESTBROOK

THE UNIVERSITY OF CHICAGO PRESS   CHICAGO AND LONDON

DAVID A. WESTBROOK is professor of law and Floyd H. & Hilda L. Hurst Faculty Scholar at the University at Buffalo, State University of New York. He is the author of *City of Gold: An Apology for Global Capitalism in a Time of Discontent* (Routledge, 2003) and *Between Citizen and State: An Introduction to the Corporation* (Paradigm, 2007).

The University of Chicago Press, Chicago 60637
The University of Chicago Press, Ltd., London
© 2008 by The University of Chicago
All rights reserved. Published 2008
Printed in the United States of America
17 16 15 14 13 12 11 10 09 08   1 2 3 4 5

ISBN-13: 978-0-226-88751-7 (cloth)
ISBN-13: 978-0-226-88752-4 (paper)

ISBN-10: 0-226-88751-0 (cloth)
ISBN-10: 0-226-88752-9 (paper)

Library of Congress Cataloging-in-Publication Data

Westbrook, David A.
    Navigators of the contemporary : why ethnography matters /
David A. Westbrook.
        p. cm.
    ISBN-13: 978-0-226-88751-7 (cloth : alk. paper)
    ISBN-13: 978-0-226-88752-4 (pbk. : alk. paper)
    ISBN-10: 0-226-88751-0 (cloth : alk. paper)
    ISBN-10: 0-226-88752-9 (pbk. : alk. paper)
    1. Ethnology—Philosophy. 2. Ethnology—United States.
    3. Applied anthropology—Philosophy.   I. Title.
    GN345.W47 2008
    305.8001—dc22

                                                        2008016691

[I]t immediately struck me that the most necessary and appropriate piece that one could possibly do at this particular moment in history would be a piece about two friends sitting and talking to each other. So Wally and I immediately began to discuss what kind of a work this could be and what might be its themes.

Andre Gregory

Contents

Acknowledgments

This book stands in numerous relations to conversations with my friends Douglas Holmes and George Marcus, but this text is not least an expression of my appreciation. No doubt I have gotten many of their ideas wrong. Just because I steal a thought does not mean I reproduce it faithfully. No doubt George or Doug or both disagree with many things I have said. They certainly express themselves differently. No matter.

My thinking in this area has been helped along, maybe sometimes unwittingly at the time, by conversations with other people who know far more about ethnography than I do. For this education I thank Dominic Boyer, Jim Faubion, Michael Fischer, Rebecca French, Lesley Green, Charles Lemert, Paul Rabinow, Annelise Riles, Sue Silbey, Tico Taussig, and Paige West.

This book is about conversation, and so reflects numerous conversations I was having while doing the thinking and writing that led to this text. Understood in this social register, however, conversation—indeed thinking—is a very diffuse thing, and so complete acknowledgment is probably impossible. One might, I suppose, genuflect toward one's community, and wave to one's friends and respected colleagues. Or one might insist on conversation in the deep and intimate sense, which would exclude virtually all professional discourse. But it is possible to draw some practical if hardly incontrovertible lines. During the time of this book's composition, I was talking about the substance of security, whatever that might be, and its relationships to that complex of mysteries called law, understood vis-à-vis very unstable conceptions of our times. In exploring these issues, Andrew Bacevich, Pierre d'Argent, Mark Drumbl, Michael Glennon, Dick Howard, Vincent Littrell, Olivier Roy, Pierre Schlag, Jack Schlegel, Frank Vogel, and my parents, Bert and Tiny Westbrook, have all said things I found important and helpful. I thank them all for their thoughts, their encouragement, and their companionship.

I admired David Brent's editorial judgment, more specifically, his boldness in an environment where lions are too rare, long before this book was conceived. His enthusiasm for this project means a lot to me. Maia Rigas has a fine ear and maybe an even better eye. She has devoted a great deal of care and good sense to editing this book, and for that I thank her. Whatever foibles remain are entirely the consequence of my bullheadedness.

Writing with more restraint than is my wont, let me say that combinations and renewal are central to my effort here, and so it would make good sense (*poeta*, making) to dedicate this book to my children, or to my wife. I love them all dearly, and my intellectual life—all these conversations—are only possible through Amy's mighty support. I am blessed. But my last book was dedicated to the children, and the one before that thanked my wife as well as I am able. I fear they are becoming rather jaded. And my anthropologist friends keep telling me that gifts are complicated things, which has certainly been my experience.

Sometimes, walking along the beach, one comes upon an elaborate abandoned sandcastle, evidently built to pass the time and to please passers-by, and perhaps worth a thought, or at least a smile, after it has been swept away. So is this book dedicated.

PART I

Into the Present

As you set out for Ithaka
hope your road is a long one,
full of adventure, full of discovery.
— C. P. Cavafy

While stringing its sentences together, I thought that telling stories was the only conceivable occupation for a superfluous person such as myself. — Bruce Chatwin

CHAPTER ONE

The Venture

This short book is meant to be read in a number of different ways:

as a sympathetic outsider's report on specific intellectual problems for some U.S. anthropologists seeking to use their discipline to confront the situations in which they (and many other people) presently find themselves;

as a response to these problems through a conceptual reconfiguration of the geometry of traditional ethnography that nonetheless aspires to satisfy much the same intellectual, indeed aesthetic, desires as ethnography has long done;

as an abstract statement of one way forward—what younger or more nostalgic folks might have written as a manifesto;

as a way of articulating broader concerns about the possibilities for intellectual life (and unavoidably, political life) under contemporary conditions;

as a suggestion of how one might be an intellectual for whom education is a form of travel writing, the life of the mind (potentially including academic life) is an adventure, and thought (even social criticism) is not just cheerful but happy; and

as the trace, if not the text, of conversation—one kind of solution.

* * *

This book presents ideas that have emerged through a threefold conversation among Douglas Holmes, George Marcus, and me. Doug and George are anthropologists, and for some years now, we have been talking about the situation of and possibilities for contemporary ethnography, conversations that easily shade into (or more truly, are required by) broader concerns regarding the discipline of anthropology vis-à-vis its institutional setting in the university, and vis-à-vis competing ways of understanding the world and our places within it. Such discussions tend to become about the university, the world, and being an intellectual, albeit seen by my two friends through the lens of their professional engagement with cultural anthropology, just as I cannot forget what I know about the law and especially the legal academy. While I have not attempted to reproduce our conversations over the years, much (not all!) of what has been said seems worth the consideration of others. So I have attempted to set forth, in general and abstract terms, some of the substance of our talks about engagements with the contemporary world—enterprises, even adventures—that ethnographers might undertake, and what such engagements might mean, both within and without the walls of the university.

*   *   *

I do not think whatever interest these conversations may have depends on the specific biographies of the conversants, but perhaps it would be helpful for me to say something about who we are. Besides, there is no point in being coy. Professionally (a word that will become increasingly problematic as this text unfolds), George Marcus, Doug Holmes, and I are all full professors on respectable if not glorious faculties. George and Doug teach anthropology; I teach law. I think the subjects in which we have been trained matter, albeit in ways I do not fully understand. Cultural anthropology (and its cousin, sociology) and law have a long history together and both depend in myriad ways on—to be unavoidably vague—social structures. But Durkheim was trained in "law" very different from that Lévi-Strauss studied, and both educations were quite different from mine. And yet there are deep affinities . . .

Sociologically, we are all middle-aged white men, well married with children, comfortably ensconced in the foothills of the bourgeoisie. For all our blessings and I would even say cheerfulness, however, each of us has been called discontent. That may be a fair description, although I am unsure what the standard of judgment here is, and perhaps our unhappiness is merely of the ordinary human sort. It must be admitted, though, that whatever unhappiness we may have tends to manifest itself as critical opposition to the status quo and, especially, as impatience with the orthodox forms that constrain us most regularly and immediately, the norms of intellectual production in our corners of the academy.

We do not understand our discontent in the usual language of revolution that, in however watery fashion, pervades the practice of critique, progressive thought, and other academic enterprises. Havel was right; revolutions are for fools. I am tempted to dismiss our impatience, especially with the academy, as merely an ingrown tendency toward disobedience, but "disobedient" is too young a word. As this book goes to press, I am forty-three years old. George and Doug are older. While each of us may be in touch with our inner child, our discontent is more middle-aged than youthful. Civility and even truth have their demands, and there is always professional advancement, but as a matter of intellectual authority, sovereigns of the mind, we find nobody left to obey or even rebel against. This is it. So what are we to make of our intellectual lives?

By this stage, one has disappointments. For instance, this book is written under the shadow of my thought that the humanists of my generation, and especially of my father's generation, have abandoned their intellectual obligations to their country, often in ways they no longer understand or have any capacity to repair. At the same time, and much more importantly for this book, one may be thankful for many things, and one may nurture hopes. So, for obvious example, I am thankful for these last five years of intellectual engagement with George and Doug, the conversations in person, over the phone, and via e-mail.

As intellectuals, we may also nurture hopes. This book was drafted with the Edwardian subtitle "Ethnography as Enterprise and Adventure in the Cross Currents of Present Situations," which was intended to echo, in rhythm and word choice, Malinowski's "An Account of Native Enterprise and Adventure in the Archipelagoes of Melaneisan New Guinea," thereby positioning this little test, written in a different key for a different time, in dialogue with the tradition symbolized by *Argonauts of the Western Pacific*. My subtitle managed to be simultaneously arcane, obscure, presumptuous, too clever by half and generally off-putting (besides, Marketing didn't like it), and so it is good that cooler heads prevailed and that this book has a rather more straightforward subtitle. I still mean to propose, however, that not just ethnography but intellectual life generally should be an enterprise and an adventure. In short, one of this book's hopes is to suggest a style for the intellectual, cheerfulness in good times and sangfroid in bad, in lieu of the moral earnestness or facile irony that are so ubiquitous. A certain levity may help us take ourselves less seriously and perhaps may enable better thought.

*   *   *

I see no need to belabor the similarity of my position, vis-à-vis my interlocutors who are official anthropologists, to the position traditionally held by the ethnographer, vis-à-vis native subjects. Nor is there any need, at this juncture, to dwell on the advantages of writing such a book from the position of an outsider.

The most obvious disadvantage of being an outsider is ignorance. I am unconcerned, however, that this book inadequately represents cultural anthropology as it is currently instantiated in the academy in the United States circa 2007. *Navigators of the Contemporary* is not intended as a description of the discipline, a sociologically accurate précis of what constitutes the field today. Again, this is a report on the thinking that has emerged through certain friendly if sometimes intense conversations, and perhaps others will find this thinking useful in moving their own conversations forward. So although there is much about institutions here, these thoughts claim no institutional authority. Professionalism may be necessary but is merely a topical concern, that is, this is not a professional effort. I am institutionally accredited elsewhere, and besides, this world has plenty of professionals. Instead, this book holds forth the possibility of an intellectual life understood to be an adventure, the collection of tales for students and professors, mostly "superfluous people" (or necessary people in superfluous moments) to retell one another. These thoughts are for fun, both at times and in principle.

*   *   *

Like memoirs, novels, and other constructions, this book stands or falls on its own. While scholastic readers may well miss the academic apparatus, this book does not argue in the conventional academic sense. By the same token, the analysis and correction of others' works are not employed as a way to set forth or legitimate my thoughts. As a bookish man writing to other bookish folks, I have been unable to resist the occasional allusion. But there are no real references here; reading other books will not make this one somehow more correct. What thoughts the book does contain are neither set forth, nor demonstrated, nor defended, in any academically forceful way. The reader is not obligated to continue; he can go elsewhere if he wishes.

I hope this lack of academic apparatus helps make the text more accessible to those beginning, or altogether outside, cultural anthropology. For those within the profession, I hope this lack makes our thinking more immediate, more suggestive, and simply more interesting.

*   *   *

Part I sets forth certain difficulties in contemporary intellectual life (and therefore institutional and political life, too) and proposes that ethnography can provide a useful, indeed an exciting, way to approach our world, a neat way to go about thinking at, and about, the present time. Part 2 explores how it may be possible to reconfigure the practice of ethnography so to address the contemporary world, while struggling to preserve much of the traditional ethnographic aesthetic, with its cognitive instability and resulting wealth of intellectual possibilities. Part 3 examines the consequences within the contemporary university of so reconfiguring, and indeed refunctioning, ethnography. Ethnography has great potential to say important things about the contemporary condition, things that are unlikely, perhaps impossible, to say from other vantage points either inside or outside the academy. Part 4 asks what this refunctioned ethnography might mean for intellectual life considered in a world in which the university is not presumed, but is itself in question. The deeper one pursues the idea of refunctioning the scene of encounter—of reinventing ethnography for our present situations—the more changes suggest themselves, problems and opportunities arise, and the consequences of the enterprise become increasingly interesting, not just for anthropologists but for intellectuals of many kinds.

CHAPTER TWO

Culture Everywhere and Nowhere

The idea of culture appears to be indispensable: in aspect after problematic aspect of our lives, answers are sought, or at least presumed to exist, under the rubric of "culture." So, in an age of globalization, one worries about the destruction of local (or traditional or indigenous) cultures, while at the same time worrying about the construction of global culture, whatever that might mean. Violent nationalisms, civil war, genocides, and of course terrorism are routinely analyzed and discussed in cultural terms. Less dramatically, the preferences, associations, habits, and identities of relatively discrete groups of people within contemporary society are discussed as if they shared an island. (Such discussions often are held for marketing or partisan purposes.) Rather than resent their designation as islanders and for sundry reasons of their own, relatively small groups of people now commonly demand treatment as cultural entities, insist on their ethnicity. And in the maw of depersonalized bureaucracies, there seems to be a dawning understanding that purely quantitative or schematic descriptions of organizations often miss important aspects of how people work together, or fail to work together, in the organization—the culture (no other word will do) of the organization seems to matter. Problems for which culture is obviously only the beginning of an answer are everywhere, and therefore, the problem of culture is everywhere.

Perhaps unsurprisingly, the academic discipline of cultural anthropology is doing well, at least in maybe superficial but quantifiable ways. Undergraduate enrollment is substantial. Graduate students continue to flock to anthropology, despite the difficulties getting teaching jobs and the lack of a well-developed nonacademic market for anthropologists, at least compared to what some other faculties within the university can provide. For all its fuzziness, ethnography is starting to be taken seriously in the business world—particularly among organizations that realize that what something means in a given social setting is not obvious. (Intel has the equivalent of a small anthropology department.) Many large organizations are opaque even to themselves; consider Enron or the U.S. Army. How such a culture works or fails to work may not be evident to its leaders, and therefore large organizations have begun to hire ethnographers. And in an age of terrorism, there is much ethnographic work to be done for those who oppose what anthropologists like to call the "other."

Despite its current popularity, however, cultural anthropology today confronts profound challenges. Consider the classic story: a young man leaves Paris or some such center for the "field," armed with a notebook, a bit of reading, rather inchoate beliefs in the importance of cultural specificity and underlying humanity, and an earnest yet pleasing manner. After some months or years of talking to, indeed living among, members of another culture, the young man returns and writes up his findings about life elsewhere—our ethnographer has mapped a culture, made it available to the world outside (or at least, made it available to Western academics). And on really good days, if our hero is a great success, then the better part of the Parisian intelligentsia will entertain the notion that they are not the center of the universe, that there are other ways of being human—that is, ethnography is always, in part, a critique of the home our young ethnographer has left. Built into this story are a host of assumptions about the modern and the traditional, the familiar and the exotic, the adventure and the objective ("science" doing double duty here), the inauthentic and the authentic, and human possibility.

This is a great story, and it sustained the academic discipline of cultural anthropology for the burden of a century. Traditionally, ethnography described the worldviews of foreign cultures. Other people see the world differently, and it long seemed (and in some places, still seems) worthwhile to describe, in relatively general, objective, and abstract language, how such particular worldviews are constructed. So anthropologists traveled and talked and found new ways of looking at life not only as it is lived in this or that corner of the map but also as life in general, even back in Paris, London, or across the rich plains of the American academy.

Living some version of this story, however, has gotten harder and harder. The maps have no more blank white spaces; the islands have run out. While there are still many different cultures, it is much harder to be sure *what* makes cultures different from one another. Life on the island, any island, is deeply shaped by national, regional, and global economic, social, and political developments. Places are becoming less isolated, and anyway, isolation is no longer any guarantor of difference. The "natives" are quite aware of their participation in larger realms, realms that include the ethnographer. One may go to Tonga only to discover people self-consciously responding to and enacting a sense of how civilized nations behave, a sensibility that was formed in many places besides Tonga. And what native might be discerned has become difficult to handle: the romantic comes to seem the Orientalist, which is too implicated with the colonial and often associated with domination, even cruelty. Once there were no more islands over the horizon of contemporary consciousness, the geographical and social context of ethnography, and so cultural anthropology, changed. It is tempting to tell this as a story of decline, the closing of an intellectual frontier, with dwindling scope for real excitement, much less heroism, the sad history of a North Atlantic intellectual encounter with the tropics.

Moreover, like other humanistic disciplines in the United States, including law, during the 1980s cultural anthropology went through a period of rupture, a substantial break with the discipline's traditions. George Marcus played an important role in making this break, and one of the functions of our conversations has been to reassess what was in fact accomplished "in the eighties," as I like to tease him. Teasing aside, he is right that there are important differences between how cultural anthropologists understand their discipline now and how they understood their enterprise in, say, 1975. The discipline to some extent reinvented itself back in the day. Cultural anthropologists underwent a crisis of faith—or a paroxysm of denial—in what they were doing. Indeed, this is sometimes called the "crisis of representation" or, more opaquely, the "reflexive turn."

Just what changed for cultural anthropologists in the 1980s remains unclear, at least to me, but nonetheless will be rather schematically discussed in part 3. For now, it suffices to say that, as is usual with periods of intellectual rupture, the university practices that constitute cultural anthropology carried on both much as before, but also differently—and what was the same, or thought to be different, remains contested long after the fact. (American law professors are still concerned with the definition, to say nothing of the significance, of the "American legal realist" movement at elite law schools in the 1930s, which was not unconnected with the birth of the contemporary regulatory state.) Indeed cultural significance, influence, is something that cannot be assessed at the time—the meaning of an argument (or a judicial decision) depends on subsequent understandings. So anthropology is still digesting the internal struggles of the '80s. It seems clear, however, that by the '90s, cultural anthropologists had internalized much of the criticisms and saw (or at least publicly explained) neither themselves nor their worlds in the traditional ways.

Twenty-odd years on, however, the internal critiques of anthropology that seemed so radical during the '80s now seem in central ways quite conservative, in the literal sense of conserving the academic tradition in which the participants had made or were at the time just beginning their careers. For all the talk about rupture, there is a great deal of continuity in cultural anthropology. Perhaps things that have been preserved should have been transformed? In sketching new possibilities, this book presumes both that there was a reconceptualization of cultural anthropology in the '80s and that this reconceptualization did not go far enough. The renewal of cultural anthropology during that period was salutary, even necessary, and there is no way that our conversations could have occurred, or this book could have been written, prior to that period of rupture. That said, this book will proceed on the assumption that the rupture of the '80s was not enough to constitute an ethnography—and so make cultural anthropology—fully prepared to inquire into many of the cultural questions that seem so unavoidable today, that is, questions raised by "cultures" of contemporary life in developed places.

Perhaps the most familiar way to use ethnography to confront contemporary situations is to replace the traditional physical geography with a social geography. From this perspective, one may maintain that ethnography is essentially an enterprise of the periphery. Ethnography thrives at the margins, where other folks are either inarticulate, outside society's interest, or even oppressed. Once upon a time (until circa 1970?) the margin could be understood geographically, as demarcated by the bounds of empire, in the colonies or beyond. But now *marginal* is defined socially, in prisons, migrant worker housing, and so forth. The fact that there are no new islands does not mean that there are no margins. There are always margins, and the job of the ethnographer is, now as ever, to report from the margins. As global society shifts, cultural anthropology simply reorients itself to begin its work, to talk to marginal people, wherever they may be found. The political purpose of ethnography, in this view, remains unchanged, that is, to rediscover the humanity in the peripheral subject. While ethnography once discovered the humanity in the "native," who, upon closer acquaintance, did not seem so unlike us, ethnography now finds humanity in out-of-the-way, often oppressed, subjects. The ethnographic tradition thus continues to intone its humanizing message. Insistence on the human is especially needful under current conditions, in the face of a dehumanizing modernity, corporate capitalism, military imperialism, rampant authoritarianism, and globalization. And so forth.

This moralizing stance easily shades into an understanding of ethnography as a form of activism or even advocacy on behalf of those at the margins, who are recharacterized as society's victims, that is, tort is substituted for space. This is another parallel between cultural anthropology and the legal academy, where in recent decades so much scholarship has been framed as advocacy for the powerless. And even legal scholarship that deals with questions that have no obvious victim to champion is nonetheless expected to make a normative argument. Much of intellectual life at the present time is, not to put too fine a point on it, preachy. So it is unsurprising when anthropology seeks to find its raison d'être and indeed identity as a discrete enterprise by way of its contribution to political discourse. In short, a chastened anthropology may still yearn for or at least claim public engagement precisely in its insistence on the claims that the marginalized make upon our humanity.

While posing as a knight-errant is obviously a tempting way to proceed, taking a marginal position as a matter of principle is also deeply problematic for cultural anthropology. Questions about what goes on at the center (not just among identifiable "elites") of the society are not asked. To insist on the peripheral is quite literally to marginalize inquiry and to miss important things at the center. In its tendency to focus on victims, cultural anthropology has rather artificially narrowed its scope.

Defenders of current practice correctly may point out that there long have been ethnographies of recognizable elites. And science studies is obviously concerned with processes near the core of contemporary society. And these days, ethnographies of the "state" are common enough. Indeed, and perhaps this is enough to ask of ethnography—but it is certainly a professionaly comfortable view of the matter. I would think anthropologists should ask whether, for example, Union Carbide is likely to be seriously considered until after industrial disaster in Bhopal, India, if then. If so, does not that tilt the field toward the periphery? Following this suspicion a bit, how many ethnographies of the state or of a given elite are conducted as critical enterprises, a form of opposition or advocacy, or perhaps an effort to speak truth to power, as the saying goes? That is, even when the topic is at the core, ethnographers often locate themselves at the margins.

But certainly exercising power is as much a part of the human condition as enduring, and perhaps even more mysterious and worthy of thought? If we turn from what questions are asked to how questions are pursued, the intentional marginalization of anthropology (and law, where this happens all the time) is again problematic. At the extreme, sympathy, outrage, and so forth tend to cloud thought. The righteous are rarely interesting. More insidiously, arguing the side of the angels makes it very easy to forgive oneself—and there are real virtues in discipline.

Such intellectual limitations might be acceptable as a trade-off for improvements in the conditions of humans at the margins. At least the lower angels need not be intellectually nuanced; they need to do good. (Lucifer himself is extremely subtle, and so his enemies must be too.) But insofar as what might broadly be called activism is the point, it is hard to see how cultural anthropology as it is now configured has much to offer, opposed to any number of other vocations, including law. Anthropology as advocacy, or public anthropology, is something of a stretch. Most of the posturing in the university is no more than that, posturing, good for the speaker, perhaps. Even in law, the potential for social redemption through right thinking and clever argument is widely and wildly overestimated. Bluntly, intellectuals of all sorts tend to operate with a naïve conception of how ideas are politicized at the present time, and so conversely, of the roles practically available to the intellectual in politics. Contemporary intellectuals are therefore regularly and genuinely surprised, not just appalled, at their general political irrelevance, an irrelevance that is to some degree deserved, as they have demonstrated that they do not understand politics.

Not to sugarcoat the matter, the relationships among argument, political activity, and the construction of culture presumed by most academics most of the time are, generally speaking, wrong. Social imaginations are sometimes formed in the university, but the university certainly has no monopoly on cultural construction, as a five-minute conversation with a student, much less anybody outside the university, would suggest. Nor does formal politics have a monopoly on cultural construction. If we shift from social space to process, one must admit that very little of cultural significance is constructed through the logic of an argument. Most of the construction of our culture takes place through social intercourse other than argument. Thus academic arguments, usually addressed to the mechanisms of formal politics, are at best quite partial.

As every lawyer or politician knows, it is the hardly rational undertones of arguments that matter, and as every even vaguely postmodern academic knows, rationality as such determines little if anything. Even where they are required and relatively rigorous, for example, in courts, arguments tend to be weak tools. There are always arguments on the other side. (The first year of law school is about the symmetrical construction of claims, that is, if the plaintiff maintains ___, then the defendant should respond ___.) Thus argument is much more a form of contest rather than a mode of resolution or construction. This reevaluation of the political significance and determinacy of argument is part of what it means to say that the Enlightenment is over, that we no longer believe our culture—no other word will do—can be rationalized in any sense deeper than formally. And academics and others who set such store in argument need to reevaluate—discount—the political significance of their disputations.

This may be troubling even if one has no political ambition. While the Enlightenment may well and truly be over, it is more than a little disconcerting to imagine a politics, more broadly, a society, in which the intellectual has no constitutive role. (The extent to which that is a fair description of contemporary politics can be left for another day.) Rephrased, our political arguments presume that culture—or at least politics and laws—are constructed, and that therefore it matters what people think. We make our own society, do we not? If so, then politics, understood as the construction of our social homes, the way we come to live, would seem to be worth thinking through. And we understandably might hope that the best thinking prevails, so that we and our children live in the best society possible. But the mere hope that the best thinking prevails is not enough, not when history shows that so much worse is quite possible.

What a politically serious cultural anthropology could offer would-be political intellectuals is a sophisticated understanding of how politics is done within a certain domain (when did this war become inevitable?). As Keynes said, we act upon our ideas, but where and how are politically operative ideas (*imaginaries* is perhaps a better word) formed? This would seem to be an essentially ethnographic question, and answering it might help to inform a more thoughtful politics. More specifically, the political challenge and opportunity for a refunctioned ethnography is to forge sophisticated understandings of how communal imaginaries are formed and, therefore, how politics are authorized in our various cultures by way of preparation for attempting to think, and perhaps even act, politically.

CHAPTER THREE

Conversation As Another Kind of Solution

Ethnography, chapter I rather vaguely asserted, promised ways to begin understanding politics in contemporary circumstances, even within the global morass. This claim needs specification, because it is not at all obvious how "politics" is to be made an academic subject. It is not that professors have not tried. Any number of disciplines purport to explain politics, and even disciplines that have no obvious relationship to politics (literature springs to mind) are forever claiming engagement, relevance, and so forth. Indeed, many, probably most, professionals in the humanities and social sciences present themselves and organize their research and, to some extent, teaching agendas around their political positions. Conferences are held, articles and books are written, dissertations proposed and defended, as "engaged" scholarship, no doubt intended to "make a difference." And if called upon to justify themselves, I suspect that most of the few academics amoral enough to indulge in projects that do not directly make the world a better place would proffer essentially utilitarian political arguments about why what they do is, in the medium to long run, worth doing. Consider, by way of examples, particle accelerators in Texas, efforts to preserve obscure species, and any number of historical inquiries.

In sober moments, however, academics ought to notice that what professors say carries relatively little weight in society writ large. While technology is important, even natural scientists are a reasonably inexpensive commodity, usually much less expensive than their equipment. Just how unimportant they are is underplayed by most academics, who in fine clerical style disparage the great unwashed. But it is hardly clear why, apart from the prejudices of our class, an academic should consider himself politically serious in a democratic, bureaucratic, or globalized market, society.

That is, the ways in which we usually imagine power to be articulated at the present time are not especially concerned with or responsive to what people like me think or do. Put more bluntly still, virtually all academics, myself included, have very little power. It is thus more than a little odd that academics as a class set such store by politics. If I really took politics seriously, I should have stayed in Washington (as a corporate lawyer) rather than moved to western New York to teach. Only a grand delusion—everybody will read my books and govern themselves accordingly—could explain my move as furtherance of my political influence. I suspect such delusions are rather widespread.

Academics (and I have to point out that I come from a family of academics, that many of my friends are academics, and so forth) seem to presume a very idealized, creamy notion of republican democracy, in which good arguments simply float to the top of the body politic. It is as if we were perpetually writing the *Federalist Papers*—we make arguments and expect those arguments to be listened to, acquiesced in, and then realized in actual politics. Exactly how this realization is supposed to take place and who is supposed to do the work are not our concerns—we are licensed idea people. Of course nobody says this out loud. Most of us think of ourselves as far too sophisticated to espouse explicitly such a high school–civics Enlightened conception of republican democracy. But the practice of, for example, 95 percent of legal scholarship, to say nothing of the essays that got me accepted into a succession of fine institutions, implicitly presume that the author is, if not Madison or Hamilton, at least Jay. (The troubling question, here suppressed, is not whether academics are as such politically influential, but instead, why do we so often pretend to be doing politics?)

As suggested above, the political irrelevance of academics is not merely a function of our society's regrettable lack of respect for the mandarin class, but is by and large substantively well deserved. Whether our polity is best understood as a democracy, a constellation of bureaucracies, or a globalized market, neither democracy, bureaucracy, nor market capitalism turn upon academic opinions or interests. The strange thing (the failure of self-knowledge) is that—so long as they are not talking about their own engagements—many academics share and elaborate these understandings of political and intellectual life. Thus the imagination of the intellectual's role in politics that dominates much of the academy—certainly law schools and, I daresay, departments of anthropology—is at best undertheorized, probably silly, and at worst deeply wrongheaded, perhaps even immoral. While a full-length discussion would take undue space, it is worth pausing to describe some ways in which any number of academics should realize that their commitments to politics as a way to organize intellectual life are at odds with their own understandings of political life.

First, epistemologically (democratically). The last hundred years—and certainly the last thirty or so—have seen a marked emphasis on the difficulties of making meaning, what we might broadly call "the turn to interpretation." In addition, we have seen a fashionable "suspicion of metanarratives," to use Lyotard's famous phrase—certainly most academics in the humanities and the social sciences will, if asked, claim to be suspicious of authority. This is all so familiar as to be banal, and I bring it up only because when it comes time to try and do politics, all this is immediately forgotten. Academic intellectuals tend to argue as if they have listeners, and not just listeners, captive audiences who are stunningly rationalistic, so that once they realize the necessity of the argument, they will change their behavior accordingly. If you only understood my argument, you would not invade Iraq, stop global warming, and nationalize healthcare. Really.

Second, bureaucratically. In a world in which power is exercised through large bureaucracies, one has to ask how arguments get heard. To whom are they addressed, and why should the addressees listen? These are not trivial questions. Professors tend to listen to people with similar credentials, employed at comparable or better institutions. Such questions of authority are not, to put it mildly, unknown in ordinary politics. "Speaking truth to power" assumes that people with power, for some reason, are listening to, and taking seriously, the speaker. But that is not a safe assumption. This is the third-largest country in the world. Bureaucracies tend to have mandates and tend to be substantively answerable to relatively few people. Assuming I am not one of those people, why would I think that institutions with power will schedule time for my argument?

This problem reaches rather ludicrous proportions in the legal academy. Law professors regularly write about the reform of society writ large, but it is unclear what the political function of such "utopian design" is. Some professors address courts as if the Supreme Court were hanging on their every word. But demonstrably, the courts pay little attention to the professoriate. What is stranger still is that most law professors, myself included, have spent time in the corporate world, the judiciary, or other centers of power. We should know better. Trying to articulate the social function of legal scholarship is a long-term project of mine, in conjunction with my colleagues Pierre Schlag and Jack Schlegel. But for now it suffices to say that the law schools have created multiple subdisciplines that are both explicitly devoted to politics and politically irrelevant.

Third, markets/globalization. A third fundamental difficulty with the kind of politics that suffuses the university stems from what we might broadly speaking call globalization. Academic political argument tends to assume an idealized republican democracy, that is, assumes people who argue amongst themselves in fairly well-defined terms about what is to be done collectively, through some set of state institutions. But we are all aware that our societies are undergoing some sort of great transformation, and perhaps the most obvious thing being transformed is the monopoly of the state upon the political imagination. Most of politics, we now see, is not done by the institutions of nation-states, and even that politics which is done by states is no longer conceived in such Enlightened terms. We thus have a mismatch between our social understanding—globalization, a great transformation—and our practice of political argument (including scholarship), which assumes an idealized republican democracy in rationalistic command of an efficacious set of institutions. More generally, politics does not provide much purpose for academic practices.

The fact that academic argument is, by and large, politically unimportant is not an intellectual disaster. The reflexive justification of book proposals, grant applications, or dissertations as political engagements is likely to be mannered, and so in that trivial sense, spurious, but so what—as a society we probably could do with a bit more politesse. On a more serious level, one of the most decisive ideas in all of philosophy is the difference in position between the thinker and the actor, the Protagorean idea that the position of the spectator is superior because it allows for understanding. That said, however, the idea that academic practice is politically unimportant poses *practical* problems for an academic like me, who thought he was reading, thinking, and writing so much painfully boring stuff because that would somehow help the republic. It turns out, the republic has gone elsewhere, and I'm an intellectual equivalent of a blacksmith entering the age of the automobile, making horseshoes for which very few horses can be found. But the analogy is imperfect. Surely thoughtful politics is not entirely obsolete? And if that is right, surely there must be a political role for the intellectual?

*   *   *

So how might we begin to think about the relationships between the life of the mind, or at least understanding oneself to be an intellectual, and contemporary politics? Instead of pursuing this question through critical analysis of academic practice, inevitably dismissing work to which my peers have committed themselves and thereby engendering bad feelings, let me use a recent project of mine to talk about the problems encountered in attempting intellectual politics, and some possible partial solutions. (I might as well deprecate myself rather than make fun of colleagues.)

As the politics of the academy came to seem silly, I stopped struggling and made my peace with sinking into the disengaged sloth that I am told can be expected of comfortable white men like myself. I have no power and little authority. I have mixed feelings regarding and little inclination toward the preaching that sustains so many of my colleagues. Life in my beautiful village is good. At the time, I was thinking and writing well, if mostly for my own understanding and the entertainment of a small circle. I was getting a lot of exercise, ski racing with the locals, building onto the house, and so forth.

My comeuppance arrived soon enough. I found myself in possession of—there was no denying it—a set of political ideas, which I think are terribly important, not to me, but to this country. And so I felt patriotically compelled to ask, how could I actually do politics with these ideas? (Patriotism is not a sentiment with which postmodern critical theorists are entirely comfortable, but there it was. While criticizing the United States (or my parents), is all too easy, they remain mine, and I theirs.) I must stress that I had no personal ambition here, at least not in the ordinary sense. My professional career was by that time already pretty much over. I had received tenure and promotion to full professor, and I had no desire for another job. Nor did I want to run for office on these ideas. Others, people who had power already and could affect policy now, needed these ideas. Let me be more direct: I wanted people who were in charge of "kinetically" addressing the enemies of my nation, that is, killing them, to imagine their world, and so their missions, somewhat differently. How to go about changing these minds? How to engage in intellectual politics, which, I had just determined, was nearly impossible, at least nearly impossible using the sorts of argument in which I had been trained and was training others? The question was not how to argue (I knew that) but how to struggle over the imaginations that inform the exercise of power in its most dramatic form, combat operations.

Perhaps the story will be instructive. Some years ago—we Americans were already again at war in Iraq—I was reading the French intellectual Olivier Roy's *Failure of Political Islam*. I understood this book quite well, but somewhat by accident—Olivier assumed certain points coincidentally emphasized by Frank Vogel at Harvard, who long before taught me Islamic law. (As a theorist of liberal modernity, I have an amateurish interest in Islamic law, which provides an external vantage from which to think about liberal projects.) I learned that Olivier had a book coming out, *Globalized Islam: The Search for a New Ummah*, and Frank invited him to Harvard to talk about it. So I went to Harvard, too—by this point I had read pretty much all of Olivier's work in English—and the three of us started talking.

What emerged from our interchange was an understanding of radical neofundamentalism as an essentially modern ideology with a complicated relation to Islamic tradition and authority. Most importantly, bin Laden's war was genuinely new, not merely in its operational structure but deep in the substance of its thought. Our new understanding of radical neofundamentalism immediately raised three timely political questions. First, why was it so hard to think clearly about this war? Second, if our description of radical neofundamentalism was even roughly accurate, then it could be forcefully argued that a great deal of U.S. policy was wrong, not just morally or legally, but also in the simple sense of unlikely to be successful. The third problem, of course, was what sorts of policies should the United States—and especially the diplomatic and security communities—adopt vis-à-vis militarized radical neofundamentalism?

Such intellectual questions posed intellectual problems, and as such, familiar work, essentially social criticism. If our task was to do intellectual politics, with the stress on "politics," however, the practical or social problems seemed far more daunting. Assuming we came up with thoughtful answers to our questions, how were such answers to be practically expressed? How would we make ourselves heard by somebody who could do something?

The most obvious way for an academic to express himself is scholarly publication. And a draft of "Bin Laden's War" was sent into cyberspace via the Social Science Research ("research" is a more serious word than "chat") Network; a slightly more polished version was published in the annual essay issue of the *Buffalo Law Review*. But such publication has to be regarded as mostly for archival and reference purposes—neither the *Buffalo Law Review* nor even the *Harvard Law Review* is "must" reading by the Dick Cheneys of the world. There is no reason to assume that such academic publication has any practical efficacy whatsoever.

It is easy to forget that, while it has always been difficult to get the attention of the powerful, in our world, overloaded as it is with information and amusements, most people need a reason to read. Good students, as well as academics, all of whom were themselves great students, tend to read reflexively, compulsively, and obediently, in order not to break the social bond, as Lyotard said, like medical doctors are said to play golf. As a result, academics often do not fully realize what an unlikely activity their own reading is. Most people do not really have to read what they are supposed to read, and in fact rarely do. Thus, in order to do intellectual politics, it is not enough to think and write well; one must give readers who have power some reason to pay attention to this text as opposed to others, or as opposed to doing something else altogether. The most convincingly written argument has no influence whatsoever if it does not reach those who can make things happen.

My next idea was to try and make a splashy "public" statement, to turn from academic authority to celebrity draw as the motivation for reading. Of course, public statements are usually made by public figures, and I was (and remain) quite obscure. But Olivier had published op-ed pieces in the *New York Times*, and Frank was at the time director of Islamic studies at Harvard Law School, so I had some hope that we could put together a statement that would be unavoidable, that would demand attention. This approach did not work either, for numerous reasons. I could not figure out, as a rhetorical matter, how to make the arguments short enough for the few important daily papers. "Punditry" magazines seemed a distinctly inferior alternative, because of the probability that our statement would be treated as more or less clever opinion, which, precisely because it was opinion, required no response, indeed no further thought, and certainly no action. By the spring of '06, however, it was clear that such problems were moot. Over drinks after a conference, it was acknowledged that the three of us were not going to reach agreement on a text, and I should go ahead and seek to publish alone. I think differences in emphasis among us could have been talked through or papered over, but both Olivier and Frank had difficulties (for entirely different reasons, some personal, some institutional) focusing on the project, and perhaps taking a nakedly political, and highly simplified, position vis-à-vis U.S. politics. And for reasons that I have already suggested, it is not at all clear that a "celebrity" text would have had much impact anyway—somebody in the *Times* critical of the government's conduct of the war in Iraq? Really?

So I began to make a third turn, from celebrity to bureaucracy. And here new conversations played vital roles. In particular, conversations on a rather idiosyncratic Web list led to a long dialogue with a scholar of contemporary Islam who, it emerged, was an intelligence analyst. One thing led to another, a proposal was made and accepted, and on November 14 I found myself at Supreme Headquarters Allied Powers Europe, the operational headquarters of NATO, addressing senior analysts on "Strategic Consequences of Radical Neofundamentalism." The talk was both critical and well received. I learned a lot from my audience, who quickly became interlocutors, about what they perceive the challenges facing the security community to be. A version of the talk appeared in a journal important within the national security community, *Orbis*. Perhaps most importantly, the NATO talk has led to ongoing conversations and a willingness to help me develop my ideas and get them expressed within other professional communities. I am not sure what difference any of this has made, but at this point I think it is fair to say that intellectual politics has begun.

*   *   *

Might something of more general usefulness be learned from this experience with "Bin Laden's War"?

Most importantly, this entire project was conceived and developed through conversation. This may sound really silly, but it is not. I am stressing the importance of conversation as a fundamental intellectual activity, as fundamental as listening, reading or other research, thinking, or writing. I am also suggesting conversation as a way to begin thinking about politics that is otherwise opaque or amorphous, a way more humane than the declaration of barbarians, which is the traditional, in Cavafy's famous phrase, "kind of solution" for holding diffuse polities together.

A colleague suggested that what are disciplines, after all, but conversations? That is clever enough, but not my point. At their best, the disciplines serve as the basis of agreement on the terms of discourse, so that conversations can grow sophisticated, even technical. All too often, however, disciplines prevent real conversation from happening by generating a predictable pseudodiscourse. Reading from a script is not a conversation. The words *bureaucrat* and *intellectual* are hardly synonymous, and while since Weber we have spoken of bureaucracies as rational, the extent to which real thought happens in a given a bureaucracy is unclear—indeed, one reason to have a bureaucracy is to routinize what would otherwise have to be thought. Once we acknowledge, with Lyotard, Bourdieu, and others, that the university is a bureaucracy, we cannot presume that thinking is going on within a given faculty or, more broadly, discipline. (It would be cruel to name moribund disciplines, which are after all still inhabited.) Moreover, and as is widely known, disciplines require specialization and, therefore, even when working as intended, tend to fragment knowledge. This is their economic and bureaucratic, and sometimes legal function—disciplines are used to create experts, who are licensed to speak, but narrowly. But many of the best conversations are with people in other disciplines or other bureaucracies, other sites of knowledge production, without license. The conversations in which I am interested are not disciplinary discourses, in a serious way, are not professional. Instead, I am interested in invitations to step outside, to cross bureaucratic boundaries, and try to communicate.

Conversation intuitively seems to be a good way to approach questions about how different sorts of people live now. To be simpleminded: if you want to know about the world of ___, then why not ask the people who live and work there, who know something? From this perspective, there is something appealing about ethnography, which has long used conversations as data. Why cannot conversations, organized in some academically respectable fashion and branded "ethnography," be used to confront, think through, the chaos of contemporary social life? If that is a possibility, then the effort to refunction ethnography (discussed in part 2) is largely the effort to think through a practice of fostering certain kinds of conversation with people who know something, or perhaps exercise power, in such a way that we learn about their world? (And just maybe, from such a knowledgeable position, might one influence the exercise of power or at least better inform it?) Can such conversational practices be, at least loosely, systematized, taught, and institutionalized? Can such practices form the basis of an academic discipline?

At the same time that I was having endless conversations about what radical neofundamentalism might mean for security, and hence our constitution, I was also having strangely overlapping conversations with Doug and George, as well as with other anthropologists, about reconceptualizing ethnography in order to make it more attuned to situations—like going to war, or perhaps derivatives trading, or the formulation of energy policy—at the core of contemporary global society. These conversations began because George and Doug were taken with my book, *City of Gold: An Apology for Global Capitalism in a Time of Discontent*, and this led to discussions of what globalization (understood as the reevaluation of established categories of thought and the emergence of new categories) might mean for intellectual life. Naturally enough for the anthropologists, but it was an adventure for me, our efforts to understand what these new categories of thought might mean led to discussions of how cultural anthropology, as a discipline, could be renewed in order to do such work. While the critiques of cultural anthropology made during the '80s rendered untenable many of the traditional positions, stances, and practices within the ethnographic tradition—Malinowski, for short—we have not seen the articulation of a new image of comparable power of what it is to do anthropology. But what if anthropology could be reimagined and turned loose upon our own cultures? At some point I realized that things had gotten a little strange. I was talking, theoretically, about refunctioning the academic discipline of ethnography even while conducting, practically, a sort of informal ethnography in order to think seriously, and perhaps even speak politically, about the current war. (As should be obvious by now, I have a lot of time on my hands.)

What I hope my experience demonstrates is that conversation—and hence perhaps an appropriately refunctioned ethnography—can present opportunities for understanding politics across disciplines and in cultural spaces that may be ill-defined or simply inaccessible. Thus conversation presents a kind of solution, partial and ephemeral, but a human response nonetheless, for the anomie entailed in contemporary, large-scale, political life, a solution far preferable to declaring barbarians at the borders.

However, not just any conversation will do. As I have also tried to suggest, many ways of talking do not get us very far in understanding contemporary politics and certainly do not help us make political interventions. I believe it is worthwhile to think in some slightly more systematic way about the sorts of conversations that might offer us the opportunity for intellectual politics. Or to put the challenge in the terms that most concern my colleagues in anthropology, I maintain that people can be trained to structure such conversations, that is, that "talk to other people" can form the basis of an academic discipline, albeit a blessedly loose one. The rest of this book sets out to theorize the sorts of contemporary ethnographic practice that seem fruitful to our questions, in ways that practicing anthropologists may find clarifying, and that other intellectuals can understand. With this theoretical structure in hand, I hope to suggest how a refunctioned ethnography can contribute to broader streams of contemporary intellectual life, for example, how we approach questions about going to war.

* * *

My efforts to think through, with a great deal of help from many friends, what bin Laden's war means for our constitution also exemplified two pieces of practical wisdom, most clearly expressed in the traditional second person, as advice. More existentially put, this book explores ways of being an intellectual—here meaning a person who thinks about a society (observes and analyzes from outside), but also attempts to participate in the construction of that society's ways of thinking, and in this way doing politics (evaluates, persuades, and participates from within)—all the while both aware of the present time, and presuming that the traditional ways of being an intellectual are insufficient. So, to be more candid, the following two thoughts have been very useful in the way I have constructed my intellectual life, and perhaps they will be existentially useful to you, too, Gentle Reader, as the Victorians used to say. Or perhaps not, in which case what I here offer as advice will serve to demonstrate some of the relations between conversation, thought, and politics that this book explores. So, for whatever they may be worth, here are two bits of political wisdom for intellectuals.

First: if you find yourself doing intellectual politics, think a great deal, but argue rarely, and only when and as appropriate.

Remember that thinking and arguing are not synonymous. Persuasion and argument are not synonymous, either. If you are trying to convince someone to do something, someone who presumably does not have to listen to you, then you should be very careful how you present yourself. Most academics, and even lawyers who ought to know better, would rather be right than effective. Learning what not to argue takes as long, and is much harder emotionally, than learning how to argue. And conversation is always much more than a logical argument, though conversation may contain argument.

Second: do not make your intellectual life dependent upon your political engagements.

Most people have other things to attend to most of the time. Real politics—as opposed to cheerleading—is occasional, unevenly distributed, and vastly uncertain, and there are many other things that matter more in most people's lives. It can be necessary to believe in the urgency, the rightness, of our own commitments, but it is also important to remember that other people have other commitments, perhaps superior to our own. As the poet Wisława Szymborska said, "My sister does not write poems."

Understanding intellectual life to be valuable only insofar as it is politically effective invites the strange combination of righteous arrogance and downright silliness that marks so much of the American intellectual scene. It is also explains much of why contemporary American middlebrow culture is neither very thoughtful nor generous. We can do better, and have in the past done better, with these matters.

But my advice to keep politics, in the instrumental or partisan senses, in its place is not merely aesthetic, not just a question of intellectual style. Understanding thought in terms of its political success (or inevitably, its failure) is a recipe for profound frustration with the world, in a word, unhappiness.

And intellectual life does not need redemption. Thinking is worth doing, even when nothing comes of it—like music.

CHAPTER FOUR

This Book and Other Books

If one took the time to ask, presumably many cultural anthropologists working today would claim that they are confronting the present, globalization, the modern, and so forth. Surely few scholars would admit that they were asking old-fashioned questions in outmoded ways. Yet academics tend to be deeply conservative when it comes to their disciplines—they have so much at stake. It is therefore unsurprising, as the preceding chapters have suggested, that much that is said to be "new" is more aptly understood as a translation of the old. And actually using ethnography to think through and write about present situations is no easy task. Ethnography as currently imagined is a somewhat awkward, if workable, tool for such inquiry, rather like using a monkey wrench as a hammer. For all these reasons, one should be skeptical of the proposition that cultural anthropology as presently conducted is fully ready to think through, and especially to communicate something important, about present situations. As my friend Mohamed Ramdane, who sells computer systems to institutions across northern Africa and the Middle East, likes to say, there is plenty of room for improvement.

At the same time, the questions asked in this book are hardly obscure, and many cultural anthropologists are in fact using their discipline to ask contemporary questions, sometimes even locating themselves within centers of power rather than on the social periphery. The entire subdiscipline of science studies may be understood in this light—as an effort to think about how the modern is constructed by people who are influential. Such efforts are found outside of science studies, too, for example, in ethnographic inquiries into the worlds of finance or military organizations. Indeed, one could explore many of the topics of this book through discussing the texts of recent ethnographies. George and especially Doug have been collecting and giving sensitive readings to a range of anthropological writings that they find in one way or another successful in addressing the present. This collection of texts, which I hope they get around to publishing, suggests strong possibilities for ethnography's evolution and demonstrates that, at least to some extent, the sort of ethnography theorized by this book is already under development, on a concrete and distributed basis. Albeit as an outsider, I understand that substantial numbers of cultural anthropologists are shifting their focus to the sorts of questions that interest me as a critic of the present dispensation and, in particular, asking questions about how power is exercised now.

Although anthropologists are in practice finding ways to use their discipline to interrogate present situations, several contemporary projects also suggest that cultural anthropology in general and its core practice of ethnographic fieldwork in particular need a clearer sense of what they are about, that is, such projects suggest that the discipline at present cannot adequately account for itself. Such projects, including this book, in one way or another attempt to articulate in general terms the practice of ethnography as it confronts our cultures. Cultural anthropology, it is evidently believed by several influential figures, is undertheorized. One must admit that, as a philosophical matter, it is difficult to imagine any practice as diffuse as ethnography being "adequately theorized," but nonetheless, this sense of needing a general theory, a sophisticated version of what in many organizations would be called a mission statement, further supports the thought that ethnography is not, at present, fully prepared to investigate the contemporary.

I have been tempted to provide a list of contemporary ethnographic projects that confront present situations in interesting ways, and perhaps another list of efforts to theorize these contemporary ethnographic projects, with of course a bit of discussion of all the works cited. I even drafted some of this text. In addition, I began drafting a listing of books that seemed significant (or at least impressive), called "Waymarks," and I was urged to write a bibliographic essay. Such references to the work of others would be intended to show that the concerns laid out here are not idiosyncratic. More importantly still, this book would silently but decisively partake of the authority of those other books. Such borrowed authority might help reassure academics that this book was worth reading, which is why I found the proposition so tempting.

It would be easy enough to generate such a survey of like-minded ethnographic projects, complete with bibliography. Actually, it would be very easy, because I personally would do relatively little of it. Instead, I would get a bunch of suggestions from George, Doug, and others, combine those suggestions with whatever was on my mind, and then set research assistants to cleaning up the text, which would then be used to show how "scholarly" my writing is. It is a poorly kept secret that such ex-post bibliographical justification is the standard way to write law review articles. Indeed, while rarely peer-reviewed, law review articles are stunningly polished (in superficial ways), because student labor is bright, diligent, and free.

In the end, however, I decided against buttressing this text with bibliography for several reasons. First, a survey of the relevant literature could not help but be misleading in terms of the genesis of this book. *Navigators* did not emerge from the womb (not to say bowels) of the Max Planck Institute or some such place, as an authoritative summation, synthesis, and advance upon the work of scholars who had gone before. This book emerged out of intense but amiable conversation, not Germanic mastery of the literature, out of intellectual affinity rather than professional authority. So to present the book as somehow the product of "research" (*Forschung*) would be to betray its spirit.

Second, again, I do not claim that this text accurately portrays or maps the field of cultural anthropology. If I did, I would have to acquaint myself with the range of work being done, that is, I would have to do a sociology of contemporary anthropology. Not only would this project be a great deal of work, but also it would be doomed to failure or at least widespread discontent. Listings are always partial, surveys inevitably cursory (or else useless). But Westbrook doesn't consider ___. Does *Navigators* get the writings of Prof. M___ right? What about the venerable scholarship of Prof. S___? Such scholarly discussions would end up being about whether *Navigators* is an accurate representation of the field, quite a distraction from asking what is to be done and what would so doing mean?

Third, supposing that the survey of the literature (inevitably) would overlook somebody's work or speak ill of somebody, or her student, or speak well of his enemy, the question would become personal, one of professional standing. But this is a game I'm not playing; I am already a professor. My thinking is neither authorized nor legitimated by the archive of academic anthropology. While George and Doug have responsibilities to their colleagues and to their tradition, I do not. I am simply expressing what I have learned and find interesting in a way that I hope is worthwhile for others.

Fourth, texts thus produced, by a kind of writing organization, are themselves bureaucratic productions rather than the representation or expression of somebody's thought. How fitting for the bureaucratic university!

(Aficionados of collaborative forms of scholarship may wish to pause and reflect here.) Whatever else it may be, *Navigators* is not a bureaucratic production. Indeed, the conversational genesis and expression of *Navigators* is intended to be a critique, at least a partial alternative, to the fundamentally bureaucratic conceptions of intellectual life that suffuse the contemporary university. But I am getting ahead of myself.

So let us assume, without bibliography and by hypothesis as it were, that the redirection of ethnographic inquiry is felt to pose theoretical, or meta-, questions. In what ways should ethnography change in order to conduct its new research? In what ways should the practice of ethnography remain essentially the same? This book sets forth one approach to the refunctioning of ethnography, but other approaches are conceivable.

Before addressing such questions, let me confront a preliminary issue: why has this book chosen the ethnographic conversation—as opposed to the artifact, or the scene of encounter, or critical reconceptualization ("concept work"), or something else—as the heart of ethnography? From my perspective, from outside of anthropology, this question has it backward. This book grew out of conversations, mostly discussions about staging, conducting, and learning through conversations. At the same time, as discussed in the previous chapter, many of my intellectual projects, including this one, are increasingly conducted as a series of conversations. And it has become clear that the right conversations, appropriately linked, can teach me new things about the world. Indeed, largely due to Doug's work with central banks, it has become clear to me that the right conversations can exemplify, situate, and even demonstrate or correct my own rather abstract thought. As also mentioned in chapter 3, I began to think about conversation as an intellectual activity in its own right. Thus my essential interest is not in ethnography per se but in possibilities for a certain kind of intellectual conversation. In the university and in the lives of George and Doug, such conversations are institutionalized in anthropology departments and discussed under the rubric of "ethnography." But those are their jobs, not mine. I am not trying to use conversation to resolve certain problems in ethnography; I have learned about ethnography because I care about certain conversations.

Were this a more argumentative book, I would maintain that conversation has intellectual possibilities that make it particularly fitting for the substantive questions that concern me and that are missed by other approaches to renewing anthropology. To be candid, however, my thinking here may be biased due to the fact that I come to ethnography largely through Doug and George, who themselves are methodologically concerned with conversation. In fact, to be very candid, I long subconsciously understood ethnography writ large as leading up to, conducting, and then learning from and communicating the substance of the ethnographic conversation (that is, the narrative of ethnography presented in this book). I have certainly engaged more deeply with Doug's and George's notions of how conversations can inform a new, more modern, ethnographic practice than I have engaged with the perhaps competing foci of other cultural anthropologists, some of whom are friends. Those things said, in ways that will emerge through this book, I think conversation is rather uniquely fitted for appropriating fragments that comprise contemporary life, as opposed to more holistic approaches—why use holistic approaches on aspects of social life known to be partial, and in that sense, fragmentary?

But this coy passage aside, this text suppresses arguments for the proposition that conversation, rather than something else, is the heart of ethnography and the key to the discipline's progress. Although I hope this book, written by a sympathetic outsider, will be useful to professional anthropologists, as a nonanthropologist I am neither particularly well equipped, nor inclined, nor have anything much to gain from arguments over whether conversation or something else would better guide the remaking of cultural anthropology and, by extension, why this book is better than other books covering similar territory. Why make people defensive, unnecessarily cause hard feelings? It is necessary to hurt feelings often enough, and besides, some of those people might assign vast numbers of this book to their students, which would be a good thing. For now, I think all can agree that conversation is important and that there is much to say, and surely that is enough for this book. (As mentioned in the last chapter, knowing what not to argue matters.)

And there is more to be lost here through argument than goodwill and book sales. Apart from cultural anthropologists, this book is written for two groups of readers—students and intellectuals more generally—who likely would be distracted and annoyed by professional sparring and who therefore might stop reading. Specific critical analyses would pull this text away from my desire to address audiences who are outside the practice of cultural anthropology but who may find this material useful to think with, or who, being students, may even decide to become ethnographers themselves. So, beyond acknowledging the fact that there are many ways to think about refunctioning ethnography, that our conversations are not the only conversations, I am going to decline this opportunity for critical analysis of alternative approaches to ethnography, and simply proceed, in part 2, to explore possibilities for and consequences of ethnography understood in essentially conversational terms.

* * *

It is also worth pausing, however, to ask whether theorizing the practice of ethnography, in conversational terms or otherwise, is a good idea at all. Not everything needs to be theorized; some things should be left unsaid. As noted above, cultural anthropologists are in fact beginning to confront the ways we live now. The fact that the confrontation tends to be undertheorized, that anthropologists have a hard time accounting for what they do, evidently poses no insurmountable obstacle to practice. But why should this be a surprise? Ever since Socrates had conversations with people who had no idea of the principles on which their work was based, we have known that a decent theory is the exception, not the rule. So is theory necessary here? Is a book like this one worth writing or even reading?

One might hope that theorizing ethnography—and refunctioning ethnography in the process—would help to improve ethnographic research. (Speculative claims of practical benefits are how abstract thought is usually justified in the United States.) Theoretical restatement of what ethnography attempts might encourage designs for research projects that are better able to reveal something important about the contemporary world. Hopes along these lines certainly animate this book. But it is wise to keep hopes modest or at least sheltered, and certainly not let what are no more than wishes be treated as if they were expectations. So, for example, it is commonly claimed that educational theory, talk about education, will make people more educated, but how often does this happen? By the same token, theory, abstract talk about doing ethnography, might lead nowhere, or to new justifications for doing bad ethnography instead of leading to brilliant illuminations. But how many teachers among themselves can resist talking about teaching? Theory has its attractions, which should be acknowledged as such—so anthropologists, as intellectuals, would like to be able to articulate what they mean by doing ethnography. Why should this intellectual impulse not be indulged? And perhaps something will be learned, and improvements will be made, after all. We can hope.

I think theory is also important to audiences for ethnographic work outside of anthropology. Students and intellectuals generally are not in a position to understand what ethnography is trying to accomplish by doing it, by osmosis, for the simple reason that they are not standing in the field. Many times over the years, I have found myself telling my friends who are professional anthropologists just how inscrutable their last statement was to me, and presumably to most anybody outside the professional discourse. But my friends' ideas are often conceived and understood within their discourse and are therefore most naturally and precisely expressed in the same language. True enough, but if one is not already a professional anthropologist, such thinking is often unduly difficult to understand. In this situation, abstract theory offers a way to make professional ideas accessible to people who do not live in the profession in which the ideas are born and have their life. Theory, in this sense, is as much a matter of translation and presentation as of thought—theory is at least as "social" as it is "analytical."

Theoretical representation of ethnography is particularly important at the present time. Cultural anthropology is still widely seen in traditional terms, as a representation of the primitive, the exotic, the other. Within the humanities and much of the social sciences, this representational function of the nonmodern continues to be useful in ways traditional since Rousseau, as either a vantage point from which to insist on the common humanity of us all, or a high ground from which to mount a critical attack on some aspect of modern society. Although such representation—and such critique—remains useful today, it does not take advantage of the essentially contemporary and internal accounts of present situations that ethnography is beginning to accomplish. Ethnographic accounts of their own world (rather than the alternative worlds represented by the other) could be very useful for these traditional audiences for anthropology, albeit useful in nontraditional ways, and theory could be used to introduce them to what contemporary anthropology offers.

Moreover, and more darkly, anthropology has been compromised by the power of nations—especially Britain, France, and the United States—in which the discipline developed. In the contemporary environment, in which security concerns are omnipresent, anthropology is again being asked to represent the other, that is, the enemy, the terrorist, and the cultural milieu that brings terrorism forth. Involvement with security raises shadowy problems for anthropology, the risk of being a tool (and a tool used to what ends?), or window dressing, or perhaps taken all too seriously, even when one is wrong . . . and yet the requests of government should not be denied automatically. Experts will be found if experts are thought to be needed. And the only thing worse than a policy informed

by a compromised understanding is, as both Iraq and Vietnam have ruin-
ously demonstrated, a policy informed by no real understanding. Thus the
fact that political understanding will always be deformed by political life,
that the *Republic* is a fantasy, is not decisive. Plato always goes to Syracuse
knowing that, from a philosophical perspective, he will fail—the question
is how, and how badly.

How might theory help with this problem? I am not sure, but at this juncture I would like to suggest that the traditional conception of ethnography—
the representation of the exotic other—lends itself to militarization. Bluntly,
such representations are easily exploited as the production of more or less
useful figurations of "the enemy." This has certainly been the U.S. experience during World War Two and perhaps especially during and after Vietnam. The current wars in Iraq and Afghanistan seem to be posing the same
need—and the same quandaries—for anthropologists. Ethnography in the
service of knowing the enemy, as a kind of intelligence, may be a simply
good thing in a war that is clearly defined and where the intentions of the
powerful are not under debate. Whether or not such wars exist, the current
wars are decidedly more ambiguous.

However necessary they may be, security deployments of old-fashioned
ethnography, Malinowski militant, what the military now calls operations
on "human terrain," do little to interrogate the exercise of power, because
they are instrumental. Nor are the counterarguments offered by mainstream
anthropologists of such deployments likely to be very powerful, in part because contemporary cultural anthropology conceives of itself as operating at
the margins. One of the hopes that suffuses this book is that a refunctioned
ethnography, concerned with the core rather than the periphery, can provide Americans with critical purchase on the exercise of their own power.
Ethnographies of present situations might serve to humanize and particular-
ize the contexts in which we exercise power and even represent ourselves to
ourselves. For a very blunt example, understanding al Qaeda as a contemporary phenomenon, a kind of modernity, might simultaneously improve
the effectiveness of the struggle against terror and forcefully remind us that
the exercise of power always raises constitutive questions for the powerful. I
have my doubts, of course—this is a lot to hope from any academic effort—
but the possibility certainly seems worth exploring.

Finally, and on a far happier note: I am told that traditionally, as well as
today, the intellectual function of fieldwork is always more than its nominal subject. The young man, or now oftentimes a woman, who goes far
away to study an academic question (even a question that could more sim-

ply be investigated in the library), is not only studying kinship among the
_____, or nowadays, the structures of NGO advocacy in _____, that
is, some question about which the entire department, perhaps the intellectual world generally, cares deeply. No, the questions that especially first
ethnographies address are important enough, again to borrow Cavafy's
image of Ithaka, to provide reasons for undertaking the journey, but they
are rarely if ever the significance of the adventure. Study land tenure;
learn about life.

From this perspective, abstract theory is quite beside the point. Ethnography is about experience, and it must be lived in order to mean anything at all. Ethnography is really an academically respectable way to let
a young thinker write his own *Bildungsroman* (novel of education), in
which he of course is the protagonist. The dissertation is more importantly
a ticket to adventure than a vehicle for or effective expression of thought.
And in this view of things, ethnography stands in opposition to theory, as
the novel does to philosophy. Indeed, theory—with its plodding logic and
endless quibbling—can only deaden the soul to the lived experience that
is the point of doing ethnography, just as ideology almost always detracts
from novels.

All this is well and good, at least for a perspective on first ethnographies done by young people. But it is a bit too romantic, too idealistically
absolute. While life may not be long, it is much longer than what Goethe
called the *Lehr- und Wanderjahre* (years of apprenticeship and wandering) in which, in our time in this context, students do their first fieldwork,
write their dissertations, and are inducted into a discipline. Over time,
hot-blooded experience and cold theory form a more complicated relationship. Many philosophical people read novels; a few novelists may even
be called philosophers. I do not believe that a theory of ethnography will
demystify and thereby destroy what is special about fieldwork. There is
little to fear from theory, certainly not the destruction of art. Theories
of ethnography (including this one) cannot capture what is most marvelous about ethnography, its sense of adventure as experienced. Indeed, it
is perhaps only from the perspective of an understanding of the limitations of thought that one can fully appreciate the wonders of setting out.
Neither Cavafy when he wrote "Ithaka" nor the speaker of the poem is a
young man. It is not that understanding fails; Cavafy knows exactly what
the young man is doing. But the wonder remains. It's a beautiful day.

PART II

An Ethnography for
Present Situations

You're on the road but you've got no destination
You're in the mud, in the maze of her imagination
You love this town even if it doesn't ring true
You've been all over and it's been all over you

It's a beautiful day
Don't let it get away
It's a beautiful day
Don't let it get away.
— U2/Bono

CHAPTER FIVE

What?

What might refunctioned ethnography, an ethnography appropriate for thinking through present situations, be? This entire book, but especially this part 2, is an effort to describe and hence loosely define at least one ethnography for present situations. Other substantive conceptions of how ethnography might be refunctioned, and certainly other formulations, are imaginable. Other conversations, like other journeys, would have produced other books. But these are the conversations Doug, George, and I have had, and therefore this is the book I have written. My task for this chapter is merely to make a start, to provide some access to the thicket of our conversations.

Any number of paths are conceivable, but let me take the troublingly self-contradictory notion of "culture" already mentioned in chapter 2. On the one hand, contemporary conditions would seem to be deeply hostile to general conceptions of culture. Less and less may one speak of "culture" in the unselfconscious way of traditional anthropology, of the way of a people, this people, with their language, their history, their ways of doing things and organizing themselves upon their land, their beliefs, that is, patterns of life spatially and temporally embedded. When the traditional ethnographer visited an island, or a nomadic tribe, he could be sure that these people, in their remote place, had their own culture—his project was to learn about the culture, understand it, and report back.

In contrast, our contemporaries do not seem to share much, not even a time or a place. Our neighbors may have different languages, understandings of history, ways of doing things and organizing themselves, and quite different beliefs—that is what it means to live in a pluralistic society. People who share an important part of their world with one another—consider central bankers, perhaps, or scientists, or Orthodox Jews—may also inhabit totally disconnected worlds. Thus a central banker may tell of the limited things he shares with other central bankers, often thousands of miles away. At the same time, our central banker may be completely different—with regard to native language, sense of history, religion, personal habits, sexual mores, etc.—from the colleague with whom he has lunch. Although our central banker's account of the world of central banking may be interesting, the substance of the account is different–generally, broader geographically, but less deep—than the sort of account required for the traditional idea of culture. The "culture" of central bankers is not to be compared with the "culture" of the Mandans that Caitlin rushed to paint before they disappeared.

On the other hand, some idea of "culture" seems necessary if we are to make any sense out of life, even contemporary life. People must share understandings of their world in order to communicate, in order to get anything done, and indeed, in order to live. We are, after all, political animals, and as suggested in chapter 2, any discussion of contemporary politics quickly turns on "cultural" questions. If we shift our gaze from actor to context, we find ourselves in much the same intellectual position. Our environment is to an unprecedented degree constructed. Living conditions in the "developed" countries are quite artificial and unnatural, which is why such countries are called "developed." Understanding and coping with a developed environment presumes we have some way of apprehending its construction, that is, some notion of the cumulative results of human efforts that we might broadly speaking call civilization, society, or culture. Thus, at just the time when cultures seem to be vanishing, the psychological and practical necessity of some version of "culture" seems undeniable.

A number of questions follow rather straightforwardly from this contradiction. What is culture, anyway? Can one speak of universal, or global, culture? Does culture have a history? One would think it must—almost any idea of history would seem to require a sense of how the character of society changed, and hence a history of culture—but if culture has a history, then what is the status of culture at the present time? And surely culture must be understood vis-à-vis its traditional antinomy, nature? But if nature is not what she used to be, what does that mean for culture? These and similar questions turn out to be quite difficult and have occasioned some very good work.

Such questions, however, need not and will not be answered here. Contemporary "cultural" anthropology proceeds without an agreed-upon understanding of what "culture" means for the purposes of the discipline.

At first blush, this might seem to be rather embarrassing. But suppose we view culture as a floating signifier, a set of square brackets, with content to be supplied in the course of the inquiry? What might it mean to take the failure to define (which is also to limit) "culture" not as an embarrassment but instead as an opportunity for learning? Has not ignorance of particular cultures, combined with the sense that each culture has something to teach about culture in general, living together, always been the occasion for ethnography?

And yet the situation of ethnography has changed, and therefore ethnography fulfills different functions, plays a different role in the theater of the mind. The traditional ethnographer was ignorant of the exotic culture because it was remote and had been rarely if ever visited by people like himself, but the traditional ethnographer presumed to understand not only culture in the abstract, but the metropole to which he reported. Today, the ethnographer knows that she does not have much understanding of her own world, whether that world is referred to in terms of the absence of culture under contemporary conditions, the continuously unfolding contemporary, the great transformation, or with one of the other current terms for the mysteries of the present situation. Confronted with our ignorance of our own situation, how might we organize our thinking, at least enough to make sophisticated conversation possible? How might we navigate our own world? This is the purpose of refunctioning ethnography.

Suppose we characterize the traditional ethnographic encounter between the native subject (in the Trobriand Islands of the western Pacific, perhaps) and the ethnographer (from London, no doubt) as a relationship, a conversation at least, from which the anthropologist will learn and upon which he will think and ultimately write. Ethnography has always been a collaboration, a social moment staged (or given or thrown) for the sake of thought, even scholarship. At least in principle, such social moments exist, or can be staged, *within* a society, not just during the encounter between what were once unproblematically called "modern" and "traditional" or "native" cultures. While it would be ridiculous to presume "to study" a central banker (why would the central banker bother?), quite a number of bankers are willing to talk about what they do. Understood dialogically, ethnographic encounters can be made to happen within contemporary settings, and indeed, more or less successful ethnographies have been done of central bankers, DNA scientists, and other actors important to contemporary society. In practice, the traditional ethnographic encounter turns out to be oddly well suited for inquiry into aspects of the contemporary.

As this list of subjects suggests, much contemporary ethnography uses identifiable groups, frequently defined by jobs, to structure inquiry. While often useful, such framing devices—substituting "expert" for "native"—are not unproblematic. Many contemporary subjects are capable of doing their own description; it is unclear that central bankers need ethnographers to tell them what it is they are doing. More deeply, the social environment in which a job is done tends to be more interesting than the job itself. The question is not central bankers but rather the environment that central bankers try to discern, articulate, and even influence through monetary policy. Rather than trying to understand experts, conversations (often but not always with experts) can be used to ask after the significance of convergences, loci and the like—collectively, "situations"—within contemporary societies.

Situations are common, and often familiarly named. Consider markets, corporations, or the state of play within any field, for example, biotechnology, in which scientists, administrators, regulators, financiers, lawyers, and others form the social environment in which new technologies emerge. Perhaps most important, politics seems deeply situated. The Beltway consensus to go to war cannot be isolated, that is, understood in terms of the agency or even leadership of one actor. Similarly, confidence in an economy, or perhaps the current German malaise, cannot be understood in terms of a well-defined actor or group of actors. Instead, these are conditions that occur within a social environment, in which various people, institutions, forces, memories, expectations, in sum, the aspects of social life, are arranged relative to one another in a particular way, a constellation at some moment. Sometimes the word "assemblage" is used to denote the specific set of relationships that the anthropologist seeks to address. Situation, constellation, assemblage—the words have slightly different associations, and sometimes one seems more appropriate than another. No matter: the task at hand is to imagine an ethnographic inquiry that fosters understanding of such hard-to-define locations in the contemporary global ocean.

In such inquiries, the "situation" plays the role that "culture" played in traditional ethnography. Like culture, the situation—our situation—is suspected, presumed to exist, as a condition for beginning ethnographic inquiry, but it is not really known. Discovering the situation and its meaning is the point of the enterprise, just as discovering the culture was the point of traditional ethnography. Therefore, shifting the object of inquiry from traditional cultures to present situations changes many things for ethnography, but it does not transform either the fundamental stance of the ethnographer or even the activity of learning through conversation—there is no need to understand ethnography as declining along with the possibility for geographic discovery.

At the same time, an island or even a tribe is a far more concrete thing than a situation, and for generations "culture" had a hard, factual quality that "situation" or similar terms like "assemblage" simply do not. Setting bounds to the situation and hence to the object of study, quite practically speaking, deciding what stays in and what is discarded, is vital to articulating anything at all. So, to continue our example, what "goes in" to the world of central bankers? National politics and unemployment numbers and orders for packaging and housing starts and the mood of business leaders and . . . and what?

Uncannily enough, in the right circumstances, the question answers itself. The ethnographic subject, for example, our central banker, must perceive himself as being capable of answering the question. A central banker has to have some sense of what is relevant to central banking—some sense of how he is situated in the social environment—in order to function *at all*. Something very like cultural anthropology is essential to operating in a society without explicit and publicly understood traditions. One may understand this linearly: society requires things of its members, and if they are not told, they must figure out what is required (or they will be replaced by somebody else, who gets it). At a deeper level, however, my point is tautological: the self and the social are mutually constitutive. So being a central banker presumes a world of central banking, and vice versa. The situation is a consequence of the actors' social functioning, often without much reference to physical location.

To foreshadow: the fieldwork with which we are concerned is largely the creation of circumstances, staging encounters, in which such understandings can be expressed and so revealed. A critical task for the ethnographer of the contemporary, the navigator, is convincing the subject to share his understanding of how his world hangs together, the synthesis of social and biographical narratives that determine his own position and through which he orients himself (we may call this an "internarrative"). As their sense of the importance of place declines, individuals must work harder to locate themselves in social space. In doing so, individuals attempt, for their own ends and with varying degrees of sophistication and self-consciousness, the same thing that anthropologists do: describe their present situation. There is an ethnographic dynamic built into the structure of contemporary life; we are all ethnographers unto ourselves.

   Insofar as it reports the already ethnographic understanding of the subject, or more precisely, treats such an understanding as its own raw material,
data, refunctioned ethnography should understand itself as a second-order
effort, as an articulation built upon the back of the subject's prior attempts
to articulate his situation. Rephrased, the ethnography of present situations
tends to be "paraethnography," at least partially defined by the prior imag-
inings of the subjects. The term "paraethnographic" denotes the ethnographer's understanding that she is using a "found" ethnography, and, presumably,
helping to occasion its further articulation. Thus the ethnographic subject is
literally a subject, a builder of the ethnography, and the ethnographer discov-
ers her topic by working, at least for a while, jointly.

   Much more will be said, but at this point we may understand the ethnography of present situations as an effort to map contemporary situations
(not cultures), through the (always already ethnographic) imaginations of
interlocutors, and as refracted and synthesized by the anthropologist.

CHAPTER SIX

Where?

In a world of fast capitalism, in which communication is instant and ship-ment very quick, place may still matter but continually must be socially specified and assessed. Geography is not so much the context within which social activity takes place; geography is more an attribute to be valued. The contemporary spatial imagination, then, even when confronting ac-tual real estate, Laguna Beach or perhaps Davos, is primarily operating in social space. The Pacific is lovely at Laguna Beach, and the Alps at Davos are indeed beautiful, but what is important about these locations is that they have reputations more prestigious than those of other places with similar physical assets. In a world like ours, where so many can move so far so easily, geographical knowledge is largely a form of social knowledge, and the question "where?" must be understood accordingly.

Place (and so distance and travel) mattered differently when the aca-demic practice of ethnography was first established. To travel from the metropolis to the periphery was necessarily to enter, bodily, a new and dif-ferent world. The islands and jungles were not only geographically remote from Paris and other metropolitan centers, but also from one another. In each place, people lived and died speaking a language, operating an econ-omy, organizing themselves, behaving in certain traditional ways, in short, constituting a "culture" in the old sense. The idea of culture, then, entailed an idea of physically defined space and of lives individually and collectively lived within such spaces, of a people upon a territory, and of consciousness formed relative to such spaces. All these things are still true, of course, but much less so than they once were. The social once could be understood geographically (people who live *here*, live like *this*), in ways that the geo-graphical is now understood socially (people who live like *this*, hedge fund managers perhaps, live *here*, in Mayfair or Greenwich). Thus traditional ethnographers could use place—this island, this area of jungle, this group of people—as a first image of culture, a way to frame subsequent conversations with "natives," literally, those who were born into this place and its ways. Malinowski's famous title, *Argonauts of the Western Pacific, An Account of Native Enterprise and Adventure in the Archipelagoes of Melanesian New Guinea*, frames his inquiry up front in geographical terms. In contrast, for this book, space is a metaphor.

Rather than being embedded in a defined place in which relationships have been established and are repeated (and one speaks of tradition), today many people move. Although personal movement is easy—we live in a time of mass migrations—actually moving is hardly necessary. Economic and other concerns shift and reconfigure relationships. (As of this writing, once again we all seem to live in the Middle East.) Even those who stay still may see their context change around them. How many places is Los Angeles, and what do the inhabitants of one know of the others? To say that one is born in Los Angeles, and is therefore a "native," conveys very little knowledge about the situation of the person in question.

A degree of caution is in order. Being born in Los Angeles does signify some things that are important, and for people located in other parts of the world, for example, Liberia, location alone might strongly imply quite a great deal of interest about that person's world. But while it cannot be denied that location matters, for very many people at present, consciousness of the frame of their own actions cannot be equated with locality—in order to understand where a person is in the scheme of things, one must ask. And in doing so, the question is not merely how are things done, in this place, but how are things being done, by whom, in this and other places—questions that may not have durable answers and that are likely to juxtapose an odd collection of significant locations near and far. Many of us live in continuously unfolding situations that are not spatially defined, though we think of them spatially and of course make endless references to places (the "Middle East" or "Wall Street" or "China") that are important for one reason or another and that may themselves be more or less well defined.

In asking after such situations, cultural anthropologists are not on an island that, however remote, remains an identifiable place with its own coordinates and indeed its own culture, and that is easily distinguishable from other places with their own cultures. Instead of landing in some archipelago, cultural anthropologists are continuously at sea, always some place, but where? Indeed, cultural anthropologists (and ethnographic subjects) are always connected with all other parts of the ocean of global society, but in what direction, at what distance, tugged upon by what great currents? The significances that constitute present situations are socially defined, difficult to be sure of, and likely to shift—it is difficult to perceive where one is. Navigation is required.

Just as geographical location is defined, triangulated, among prominent landmarks, the navigator attempts to locate her inquiries vis-à-vis various features of the social topography, features that ordinarily may be considered disparate. In an effort to define present situations, ethnographers may triangulate among disparate points that establish a position, form a meaningful whole, as they are considered vis-à-vis one another, as a navigator does for her boat. Nobody individually represents a contemporary situation; no single reading establishes a position. Multiple internarratives brought into conjunction, however, may be seen to represent (mimetically) the structure of a contemporary situation. Thus, for the navigator, her interlocutor does not so much transmit the map of culture as provide data that can be used to help determine where the navigator herself is, much like the glow from Havana's lights over the horizon.

The ethnographer of present situations must be not only a navigator but also a trader. She brings different structures into intellectual conjunction. The ethnographer intentionally mixes ideas, mirroring the social mixing of contemporary life. To exaggerate only slightly: in the design of contemporary ethnographic studies, everything depends on marking out the multi-sited mise-en-scène across which discourses, knowledges, histories, and practices are conveyed. This book proposes conventions for thinking through such designs, that is, for staging certain kinds of conversations. Experience suggests, however, that such conventions are usually rather fairly fragile arrangements, polite in a number of senses—other relations soon emerge, and the discernment, analysis, and expression of these newly established relations constitute much of the real, unconventional, and hence somewhat impolite, work that ethnography does.

Refunctioned in such terms, ethnography may operate outside the conceptual bounds of the nation-state that tacitly informed traditional ethnography. Insofar as a culture was understood to be the lifeway of a people upon a territory, and especially insofar as the dark temptation of ethnography was conceptual or actual complicity in nationalist projects of colonization, then traditional anthropology tended to bifurcate its subject matter (usually silently) between cultures that would disappear before more successful nations (or perhaps would be preserved on reservations), and cultures that would modernize, determine their fates, and become nations, formally expressed as states. But the paraethnographic reliance of contemporary anthropologists upon their interlocutors' internarratives, combined with frankly multisited inquiry, in which anthropologists reckon their location among a collection of perspectives, suffice to establish the parameters of present situations within social spaces that need not depend on the nation-state. So, for pointed examples, ethnographies that sought to articulate the worlds of WTO officials or al Qaeda operatives, or to chart the market for uranium enriching centrifuges, would necessarily concern themselves with various states—but these situations would not be delineated by, nor be reducible to, contemporary or ideal national boundaries. New maps are possible, indeed necessary.

*   *   *

And yet cultural anthropology retains from its scientific heritage a certain watchfulness. (I am using "science" in the broad sense of *Wissenschaft*, that is, nothing like a *Two Cultures* critique is intended here.) While it would be naïve and philosophically untenable to maintain that ethnography offers an Olympian perspective on, or an objective representation of, Truth with a capital "T," ethnographers tend to be observant, and usually critical. They presume to have seen, and therefore, to be able to judge. Notwithstanding the vaguely postmodern stance anthropologists reflexively adopt when asked metaphysical questions, cultural anthropology is done from a shoulder, if maybe not the summit, of Mount Olympus. The ethnographer is always somewhere else, watching, evaluating. A certain kind of intellectual automatically invokes Benjamin's *flaneur*, the man walking through a somewhat foreign city with which he is intimately familiar. For now, it suffices to insist that the ethnographer is never fully here.

This distance between ethnographer and subject is neither accidental, nor merely an aesthetic stance common among cultural anthropologists, nor some sort of trace of the aspirations to hard science within the cultural anthropological tradition. The academic may sympathize with his subjects, but so long as he remains an academic, he is never fully engaged. To be crass, the academic confronting present situations always has another income, another point of view, a different source of social status. As I sometimes try to tell my students, law school should not go too far in mimicking practice in the "real" world (meaning the world of government, corporations, law firms, any large bureaucracy besides the university) because, at least for students, the law school cannot be the real world. Students are neither licensed, nor responsible for others, nor trying to establish themselves autonomously. The intellectual context of intellectual life can be deemphasized but not eliminated altogether—ethnography remains an academic pursuit for the simple, but sufficient, reason that it is conducted by academics. For professors, the trick is to capitalize upon the academic perspective, not to pretend the perspective is not ours, not to deny that we are in fact academics.

Oddly, Bourdieu and others have worried that the academic perspective is vulnerable and needs to be protected. More specifically, it has been said that the special virtues of the academic perspective might be compromised by adopting the intellectual frameworks, discourse, and justifications of the social practices under investigation. In this nightmare, cultural anthropology loses its specific intellectual authority and simply shills for other cultural discourses. Such fears are not completely unfounded, as discussed in the next chapter, but are somewhat overwrought, like worrying about the ruinous effects of the perfect marriage upon one's individuality. The academic can afford to be standoffish, indeed cannot resist exercising the autonomy afforded by having a secure position elsewhere. As grubby as struggles within the academy can be, vis-à-vis the rest of the world, the cultural anthropologist is like a London gentleman with an income from a property. For ethnographers, the conflicts and questions raised by present situations are interesting, maybe even fascinating. For people in such situations, the same questions are likely to be existential, maybe even vital to their survival. The anthropologists' perspectives are "academic" and fundamentally different from the perspectives of their subjects. Loss of a scholastic perspective is hardly an issue. (Whether the scholastic perspective is worthy of respect is a different, and much more threatening, question.)

In his interested yet relatively disconnected state, the academic anthropologist recapitulates, in an economic register, the geographic imagery so traditional in anthropology, the ethnographer as traveler. That the traveler tended to be a gentleman of means is precisely the point. Ethnography's commitment to the object of its inquiry, now as then, is less than total, and therefore free to be rather purely intellectual. The ethnographer does not want (should not want) to go native, to become an islander or a genetic engineer. But as a result, the ethnographer may be able to think and is almost certainly able to say things that people who are completely embedded cannot. Distance—not being completely there—can provide perspective and freedom to speak.

CHAPTER SEVEN

Who?

Refunctioned ethnography has a more complicated cast of characters than the conversations traditional between the ethnographer and native subjects or informants. In contrast to the bilateral encounter over a camp table, ethnography for present situations is normally if not invariably constituted by the *ethnographer,* multiple *subjects* in some relation to one another (what relation may be self-evident or may have to be discovered by the anthropologist), and *liaisons.* The contours of ethnographic fieldwork are determined by the relations the ethnographer establishes with the liaisons and the subjects who provide the material critical to the construction of her project. Rather than a sequence of interviews, refunctioned ethnography is much more like what in theater would be an ensemble production, which works through synchronization, or perhaps better, a film montage, in which relations among disparate and apparently disconnected items are established.

The navigator is likely to confront several formidable obstacles in her efforts to initiate conversations—take readings—that will allow her to chart her situation. Her subjects may well be very busy, and with no particular need to discuss their views with an anthropologist, especially some graduate student. Moreover, and particularly as ethnography is done across sites that are central to the functioning of contemporary society, subjects tend to be more experienced, and at least as well educated and intelligent, as the ethnographer. Unlike the traditional ethnographer, the navigator ordinarily has little authority, scientific or otherwise, when she seeks to talk with members of any number of today's elites. To make matters worse still, because her inquiry is essentially dependent (or "paraethnographic"), the navigator relies on the subject to constitute much of the inquiry. Without a regulative idea of culture that might be used to structure her project, the navigator has only a vague idea of what she is studying—the idea is that her project will (in common with much serious writing) find its form as she works through it. In designing and undertaking her project, the navigator relies on the ethnographic process, specifically on the willingness of her subjects to delineate their worlds, to help her more precisely conceptualize where her own work is going.

The navigator's reliance upon the subject for guidance gives rise to two broad classes of problems that must be guarded against, namely, that subjects will talk too much or not enough. It may seem odd to think of a subject talking too much. But some subjects will intentionally (or not?) seek to establish a conversational space and invite the ethnographer into that space. The subject will suggest that the ethnographer and the subject already share a situation, and the "subject" (who has come to control the conversation) will help the ethnographer to see it. Through what we have sometimes called "intimate artifice"—intimate because it seeks to position the ethnographer (now the listener, not the questioner) within a world, "artifice" because the world is constructed right there, in the ethnographic encounter—the subject may seek to beguile the anthropologist (and who would not be preferred to be written up by a fan?). Politicians and journalists often unselfconsciously evoke the familiar, which may be profoundly comforting for the navigator, who is by hypothesis at the edge of lost, at sea. So Le Pen conjures an idea of "Europe," of course his idea of Europe, but if you think about it, perhaps you will discover that you have already agreed? Obviously, this can be enormously helpful, because the subject becomes a teacher and introduces the navigator to the world about which she may write. But at some point, the ethnographer is no longer navigating but is instead being steered.

As exhilarating as such encounters can be, and as much as they can teach in a hurry, they are obviously deeply problematic for an ethnography of present situations. The problem is familiar from critiques of the Malinowskian encounter, in which the informant (often presumed to be an ideal informant) orally describes and thus represents his culture to the ethnographer. But the traditional ethnographer had no assurance (what assurance could there be?) that the informant's representation was true or even fair, rather than biased, ignorant, diplomatic, or even malicious . . . How was the ethnographer, a stranger on the island, to evaluate the representation which formed the basis for his own representations, in his scholarly writing? And a great number of anthropological controversies over the years have involved claims that famous ethnographic representations were profoundly, and often unwittingly, biased or just ill informed.

For refunctioned ethnography, the problem is if anything more acute. Paraethnography always risks becoming merely parasitic and derivative precisely because refunctioned ethnography is structured to be open. The navigator brings little knowledge to the table and seeks the knowledge of the subject. But the subject knows what he is talking about, and the ethnographer does not. Curiosity implies ignorance and therefore vulnerability. In such situations, and as will be discussed in more detail below, the ethnographer must guard against becoming a sort of shill for the perspective of the subject, which at best would be intellectually superfluous. Although the subject has a worldview, and this worldview is absolutely indispensable, the point of doing an ethnography of present situations is to articulate the *situation*, not merely to record an individual's worldview (to provide the description of a perspective), which would in effect be a form of biography. At least some subjects are more than capable of writing their own memoirs.

In contrast to the subject who seeks to dominate the encounter, and perhaps more commonly, many subjects do not talk enough. They may not have articulated, even to themselves, their own sense of their situation. To know where one is, to find one's way, and to be able to draw a map or give directions, are different things, in social as well as in geographic space. Even the subject who is capable of drawing a map may feel no obligation to help the ethnographer, or even that helping the ethnographer—explaining how things "really work around here"—is likely to leave the subject vulnerable, or is a betrayal of one's peers. People speak off the record for a reason. Thus a recurring problem for refunctioned ethnography (indeed, for classical ethnography and for journalism), is to get subjects to open up, to share what they know.

Experience suggests that subjects tend to think in general terms about their situation if they themselves are somewhat withdrawn, even marginalized. People in the thick of things have little time to think and may be unwilling, or even unable, to articulate what they actually know in some form that the ethnographer may use. Such people often justifiably believe that the consequences of their speaking may threaten or distract from their enterprise, or may impose other costs, even make enemies. For all these reasons, central figures are not the best subjects. What a CEO, a politician, or a general says about their enterprise is always already a public statement, more or less scripted, and therefore somewhat suspect.

Subjects also tend to think about their anxieties. Successful conversations often begin with the ethnographer conveying to the subject the sense that the concerns of the subject are at least partially understood by the ethnographer. Ideally, the ethnographer becomes a sounding board for the still fluid thinking (as opposed to the public projection, the shtick) of the subject. The resulting account of the subject's anxieties gestures outward, toward the space that the navigator herself is attempting to conceptualize. The subject's expression of the threats and problems entailed in his world permit the navigator to chart the environment of these problems, that is, the situation that is also the subject of the ethnographer's inquiry.

The subject's image of a situation is, by definition, based upon views from the subject's perspective, or perhaps the subject's imagination of other possible perspectives. As discussed in the previous chapter, one cannot navigate with only a single waymark, and therefore multiple views are required. Rephrased, contemporary ethnography tends to be multisited. The ethnographer must stage multiple conversations, with different subjects, positions (physically but especially socially) different from one another. The function of the ethnographer conducting a multisited inquiry is to weave into some sort of meaningful whole the various things understood, some no more than flashes of insight, acquired among notable, even singular, encounters.

As a result and in general, the multisited character of ethnography for present situations means that the ethnographer will not grow into the practices of a specific place. Sailors are not settlers. In contrast to traditional ethnography, the "thick description" valorized by Geertz and others, contemporary ethnographic encounters will tend to be relatively "thin," even anecdotal. Multisited ethnography thus runs a substantial risk of superficiality, or even failure to understand at all, and much of the skill of conducting contemporary ethnographic research will hinge on knowing when enough is enough, and when deeper immersion is necessary. For example, for an ethnography of computer scientists presumably some facility with computer science is required—but how much is a question of scholarly judgment. And many things entailed in "thick description" can be ignored. After all, present situations encapsulate far less than all of culture, and the subject is not talking about his life in the round, just about what he thinks about the situation under discussion. Therefore many things of concern to cultural anthropology, and presumably even to computer scientists, are likely to be outside of a given paraethnograpic project. Issues of kinship and burial rituals and much else that is human are no doubt engaged by computer scientists, too, but are not distinctively found among computer scientists.

Multisited ethnography is likely to require an entrée. Access to important subjects is often difficult. The time that both the subject and even the ethnographer can expend upon the project is relatively short—contrast the native subject, who speaks for hours, oftentimes days, and over the space of months or years. Can one imagine the principal investigator in a major research project devoting so much time (any time?) to an ethnographer? Such conversations might happen, but it is hardly obvious that all the parties involved will recognize that they should happen. As a practical matter, for an ethnographic conversation to take place, with many subjects in many situations of interest, it will often be necessary for somebody to act as a liaison between the ethnographer and the subject. A liaison understands something of the subject's world and something of the ethnographer's project, and is in a position to convince the subject that this ethnographer is worthwhile. A liaison introduces the ethnographer to one or more potential subjects, and facilitates the conversations at the core of ethnography. Obviously, a multisited ethnography may have more than one liaison.

To summarize: conducting an ethnography of a present situation warrants the establishment of a set of relationships. The ethnographer who wishes to learn about present situations should expect to undertake multiple, essentially triangular, negotiations to produce ethnographic conversations. Or, to shift imagery: taken together, such encounters produce a conversational fabric, woven from negotiations among (and generally in this order): the ethnographer and the liaison; the liaison, on behalf of the ethnographer, and the subjects; and the ethnographer and the subjects. This is the *Stoff* (both fabric and literary material) of ethnography, cut and stitched together to produce a scholarly account, the emperor's new clothes.

CHAPTER EIGHT

When?

Ethnography for present situations is, obviously, concerned with the present. The present may be thought of as simultaneously a vantage point and the time under investigation. Since a vantage point is invisible to one standing on it, refunctioned ethnography tends to pay attention to the near future and to the recent past in order to approach the present infinitesimally. So the present may be thought of as the starting point for speculation or as the limit, endpoint, of history. Every moment, including this moment, has a temporality.

The future may be "merely" speculative, but a moment's reflection suggests how psychologically ubiquitous the future is. All hope and all anxiety, and for intellectuals, most argument, and so a great deal of mental life, are directed toward the future. Unsurprisingly, subjects' views of the future color their views of the present; the near future is entailed in our experience of the contemporary. But if the anticipated informs the now, brings the future "back" to our present, the incomplete projects this moment "forward" into the future. To be present is to be on the scene, now. But something that is present has been presented or has just arrived, and has not yet arrived completely, will continue for at least some time into the future. The present situation is always the situation of the moment after this one. The present danger has not yet occurred. The danger is present, the harm is anticipated, and in the next moment, the danger will still be there. But the worry is here now. The same point may be made sociologically. Important contemporary enterprises tend to be obsessed with that which is invested, that which is under development, that which must show results soon. The temporal preoccupation of finance and of applied science (and all commercial science) tends to be the near future. What will happen? What are the risks and opportunities? What is to be done?

The recent past may also be a fruitful emphasis for an ethnography of present situations. This may seem surprising, since the already completed is no longer obviously present to our minds except as a memory. But upon reflection, the past is everywhere: the artifacts of our world, the structure of our thoughts. And that which is completed may be understood, which is a comfort. The media tend to report situations that have coalesced, that are already understood within some received frame of reference, often even a narrative. But what was really completed? When did the war become inevitable? As Faulkner said, the past is not prologue—it is not even past. We are haunted by the unfinished actions of the past, and therefore we need a history of the news.

The same dynamic is at work among even our academic ideals. In arena after arena, we are confronted with clichés, prejudices, beliefs about the world, consciously articulated fragments. One might think, in an information society, that such things could be derived from texts, but often this is untrue. The sources of belief tend to be diffuse and obscure. There is no canon, or the canon exists but is unread. Consider widespread beliefs about bureaucracy (but who reads Weber?) or liberal economics (ditto Adam Smith). The present is understandable only in the context of conceptual frameworks that arise . . . somehow, and then become common knowledge, obvious. At which point, oftentimes, they are rewritten.

Thus the "present" with which ethnography of present situations is concerned contains (or concentrates) a narrative. Conversations may be about how things are now, albeit a "now" that is constructed over against ideas about what the recent past and/or the near future mean. Ethnography for present situations attempts to identify, articulate, and interrogate the emergent—that which is coming out of our past and shaping our future but which we must cope with right now.

*   *   *

Cultural anthropology is so interesting, even dramatic, in large part because of the tensions and outright conflict among the different temporalities of the various narratives that comprise ethnographic encounters. To be schematic and familiar: the time of the native in a traditional society is not equal to the time of the traditional anthropologist (Malinowski) writing for a modern society is not equal to the time of the scholarship itself. A great deal of intellectual work is required to understand, albeit often only implicitly, such temporalities and relate them one to another within a text. Even though often embedded in the work done by very academic intellectuals, there is something profoundly moving about the interplay of different senses of time, which we may encounter as individual human narratives (which make claims upon our sympathies), or abstract as conceptions of history (which make claims upon our loyalties). For other intellectuals, and perhaps anthropologists themselves, much of the drama of anthropology arises from the fact that the scene in which anthropology occurs is inherently unstable. It is uncertain how things will come out, but it matters to the narratives through which lives are framed and have meaning. So we contemplate Boas sending out his students to study Native American tribes, before it is too late . . . and we think.

The drama presented by the anthropologist's articulation of conflicting temporalities in the world gives rise to another, essentially intellectual, narrative, the ultimately futile struggle of the anthropologist. The anthropologist always fails to manage the temporalities with which he is presented because success would require not only theories of cultures but also theories of modernities both achieved and merely plausible, and some grammar with which such things could be interrelated and then explained to people who did not already understand. But perhaps it makes no more sense to speak of the failure of anthropology, in this sense, than it does to speak of the failure of even the greatest of novels to make other novels irrelevant.

As already suggested, cultural anthropology traditionally involved at least three quite different temporalities, which are worth a caricature by way of backdrop. First and most obviously, native culture was understood to be significantly if not entirely outside of time. Within the tradition, the past was much like the future, and historical change was deemphasized. Native subjects often helped by understanding their cultures rather ahistorically, as having existed since time immemorial or at least since the long-ago beginning. And such cultures were expected to continue pretty much as before, to operate within the tradition, until the end time, however that might be imagined.

The anthropologist, in contrast, made his career in a society that understood itself to be progressive. Tomorrow would be different in kind from today, which was already different from yesterday. The modern world was categorically different from traditional cultures, not this or that society, but traditional cultures in general, because the modern world had dispensed with the idea of an overarching tradition, or at least was continually reinventing its traditions, in an evolutionary progression. Indeed, the cultural anthropologist himself, who contributed to the cumulative store of knowledge ("science") was a mechanism of such progress. If traditional cultures were stable, static, atemporal, and ahistorical, then modern societies were unstable, dynamic, progressive, and historical.

While history was difficult to understand in any detail—consciousness of becoming modern required not just the academic discipline of history, but also made it necessary to have theories of history, none of which has proved very satisfactory—history was widely believed to follow some basic rules. The first was that history was a linear affair, like a train that moved inexorably forward along its tracks if perhaps not always at the same speed. Another great truth about history was that the modern and the traditional were incompatible. When the modern came into contact with the traditional, the traditional would succumb and become modern. That was part of what it meant to be modern in the sense of avant-garde, the first of what soon will be normal, simply the way things are done.

Within modern societies, the dominant opinion seems to have been that history, thus understood, was a good thing and that it was good to live in a progressive as opposed to a traditional society. There was always an articulate opposition to such boosterism (consider Rousseau or *Franken-stein*). But for many years, even those who found much of "progress" distasteful or even ignoble seemed to think that whatever progress might be, it was inevitable, that tradition was doomed and all societies would become modern.

The third temporality was that of scholarship. Strangely like traditional societies (but different!), science was assumed to exist rather atemporally. The true statement—that is what science does, generate true statements— is true without regard to the time in which it is made. Two plus two always equals four. Admittedly, there were conflicts within science, and sometimes time mattered: later statements were generally regarded as more authoritative than prior statements. The Copernican view replaced the Ptolemaic one. But this was usually phrased thus: the Copernican view became the scientific view, that is, (good) science was (by definition) true, and therefore atemporal.

To repeat, this is a caricature of traditional cultural anthropology, but it should suffice as a reminder that cultural anthropology is now conducted on very different conceptual terrain. Indeed, cultural anthropology did much to reshape the intellectual landscape in which it now works. So, for a familiar example, it was a special service of anthropologists to ask what widespread assumptions of the inevitability of progress might actually mean.

Upon inspection, many traditional cultures seemed to resemble "modern" societies in important ways. Conversely, many things which were thoughtlessly considered "modern" seemed to be quite deeply rooted in traditional cultures. The division between modern and traditional grew less clear, and so the idea that the traditional would somehow "give way" to the modern came to seem an unduly primitive conception of social change. For another example, cultural anthropology tended to see truth systems as products of the society in which they were developed and used and consequently informed by that way of life. Why should our society and its truth systems, most especially the sciences, be any different? All this is familiar—the modernist *Weltanschauung* within which cultural anthropology was developed and which the Malinowskian project expressed, sometimes beautifully and even tragically, came to seem implausible, and cultural anthropology itself was one of the reasons why.

To be more specific: if we revisit our three temporalities (the traditional/ahistorical nature of the subject; the progressive/modern temporality of the anthropologist as member of society; the atemporality of science) we see that all three have changed. First, many contemporary subjects of ethnographic inquiry are, like their ethnographers, operating within a contemporary global context. Indeed, ethnographers of present situations are often drawn to dynamics that seem to be influential, to cause significant change, and therefore to be veritable motors of change. Between the ethnographer and the DNA scientist, who is more old-fashioned? Thus, rather than the contrast between "traditional" (subjects) and "modern" (anthropologists), contemporary ethnography is more likely to be drawn around contrasting stances, between instruments of change, perhaps agents (subjects) and observers or commentators (anthropologists, or subjects in an anthropological mood, what we call paraethnographers). Within this dynamic, contemporaneity (like modernity, but more doubtful) is assumed, and recognized as something of a mystery.

Second, the temporality of the anthropologist is no longer so clear, in part because the bifurcation between traditional and modern societies is no longer so clear. "Traditional" societies seem to meet changes in time, and so become modern. And "modern" societies appear to be suffused with tradition. By the same token, the concepts of "culture" and that which destroys culture (the rational, modern, or global) have not stabilized much. As with many other large concepts, we may know what we mean in a given context (and so can say this is more modern than that, or this is Chinese, rather than Indian, in cultural origin), but comprehensible usages do not mean that we have understandings that are simultaneously abstract, precise, agreed upon, and worthwhile. As a result, the idea of the "modern" has shifted. Modernization seems less unified, less inevitable, not clearly good (nor bad), and in some strange way, less significant than it once did. (I have even argued that each of us employs multiple and contradictory understandings of "modern" in our everyday evaluation of social narratives, and hence political and legal thought.)

Third, science, including the ethnographic corpus, has come to seem much more of its time. In particular, the work of anthropologists (and other scientists, even natural ones) is now understood as responsive to particular circumstances, undertaken for contingent reasons, in questionable ways. Dramatic examples are provided by wartime funding of useful area studies, but more generally, inquiry is understood to be undertaken by people who have reasons for being interested in certain questions as opposed to other questions.

*   *   *

Much of the interest and critical power of classical cultural anthropology was generated by the tension between the traditional and the modern, with a none-too-subtle undertone of innocence lost, the garden and the sorrows. The guilt of the modern was never very far away. The intellectual situation has changed, but the sensibility has remained much the same. Ethnographies of present situations ask what is this modernity, and implicitly, what was lost when this version of the future was chosen over some other version. The guilt of the modern is still not very far away—and this sense of complicity, even sin, gives contemporary ethnography its critical, even political, edge.

CHAPTER NINE

How?

The foregoing chapters suggest how ethnographies of present situations might be conducted, and in doing so, the text suggests how the enterprise of ethnography might be reimagined. What is needed, or at any rate what I can hope to provide in this book, is not so much a new practice of ethnography—that is already under development by ethnographers in the field—but a fresh and understandable statement of what it is to do ethnography, and thus a new image of what it is to be a cultural anthropologist.

Can we create a general narrative account, something less than a template, of how conversational ethnography is done? One might begin by considering ethnography in three basic phases: conception (education); research (ethnographic conversation); and expression (creating an authoritative text). (This same division will be used to structure much of part 3.) Conception is difficult to articulate further and in the abstract, but in some sense, it is always an engagement, indeed a struggle, with the establishment, easily exemplified or personified as a recapitulation of the teacher's career. Students have their own needs; the teacher responds with what he already knows. So the beginning student is fed a diet of conceptual vocabulary, what law professors would call "blackletter" or hornbook lessons. Kinship is ___. As the student advances, mechanistic conceptualism is replaced by serious texts, under the motto "one ought to have read ___" (if one is to consider oneself a cultural anthropologist). Such superficially dictatorial pronouncements, however, tend to be based on deep acculturation. A professor knows, in many ways and even if he knows little else, what it is to be a member of the profession (guild), and why his student is not to be taken seriously (except as a student) yet. More or less systematically, the teacher probes the ignorance that keeps the student from being counted among those in the know, and more or less systematically the teacher remedies his student's shortcomings.

Once the student reaches the stage at which it is necessary to conceive an ethnographic undertaking of his own, then the teacher becomes more of a mentor, on the basis of his more experienced and generally more sophisticated anticipation of what might work, that is, what course of research might generate something interesting enough to form the basis of a professionally acceptable (defensible) text, and what is likely to fail, that is, lead to something uninteresting, unachievable, or worst of all, embarrassing. Thus, in the conception phase, and even if not entirely obviously to the student, pedagogy is guided by a rather inchoate but very strong idea of what might generate a report on the "world," that might be viewed favorably by the profession's cardinals. And at some point, the student becomes credentialed in his own right and on his own. As the teacher falls away, the scholar still considers the question, no longer personified by the teacher (instead, personified by the advocates of [stupidly] received opinion and [undeserving] rivals): is this, professionally, a question worth pursuing? An ethnographic research project thus has its prehistory in the discipline, which may be abstractly presented as "theory" but which the student experiences as his education, and the practicing ethnographer as the effort to formulate and pursue a question that is of interest in the profession or, at least, that can be answered in a way that will be at least aesthetically appreciated by elites within the profession. Ethnography always begins before it begins, in the effort to plan a worthy project.

*   *   *

Once we move from theory to research, from planning to doing the project, and ethnography proper begins, then the task of the ethnographer is to make sense, build meaning, out of the material produced by her own ethnographic encounters. We are especially interested in conversations. Obviously, each fieldwork project develops in its own way—no two trips are the same, that is a vital point—but a few general remarks may be made about the conditions under which ethnographies of present situations are commonly done. Subjects are generally busy; ethnographers are likely to be relatively unimportant to them. Moreover, the ethnographer oftentimes would like to initiate a conversation on the subject's concerns or anxieties. As a result, initiating conversation is likely to involve substantial negotiation. Indeed, and especially for ethnographies involving subjects who are socially important, successful negotiation may require a go-between, a liaison. Thus the negotiation with the ultimate subject is preceded by a negotiation with the liaison; the ethnographer faces a succession of negotiations.

Once the ethnographer gains access to the subject, however, the conversation has literally only just begun. The ethnographer must encourage the subject to "open up" and share his perspective, the sense of connections that forms the substrate of paraethnographic articulations of present situations. Thus negotiation is followed by evocation. Eliciting the subject's ethnography is likely to be spurred by a sympathy for, or at least some cognizance of, the subject's concerns. And here the anthropologist's status as an outsider can be a real asset. Certainly, the outsider is ignorant. But the outsider does not have to pretend to knowledge or compete for expert status. The outsider is free to be a fool (and hence to become wiser). Even in the course of conversation, ignorance can be turned into an advantage—people often want to talk about their worlds, and talking to an outsider forces them to step back and try to think clearly about what is important.

People often want to talk—this point cannot be emphasized enough. It would be easy to argue that loneliness is the default position for so many people, and that so many contemporary phenomena, from the hunger for celebrity to the willingness to talk to cultural anthropologists, should be understood as responses to loneliness. But it might be more generous to say that folks want to explain what makes their worlds work, how they understand the forces that make things happen, things that are important to them. Thus, if they believe that the ethnographer genuinely wants to learn what they know, if the conversation is *about* something, then many people really do want to talk. The facts that the ethnographer has little knowledge, is actually quite ignorant, and has no institutional authority, can be minimized if the ethnographer can establish a substantive intellectual link with the subject. The ethnographer's goal, therefore, is to begin a conversation that not only cuts across the various disciplines represented by ethnographer and subjects but that also makes such disciplines almost irrelevant. Disciplines will never be completely irrelevant—it is where somebody is "coming from," so to speak—but disciplines can and should be minimized.

Even subjects who speak, however, may not speak clearly. In particular, insofar as they are speaking to graduate students who are (by and large) fairly ignorant of the world they are studying, the subject's discussion of the world may not be cognizable by the student. In the traditional encounter between cultural anthropologist and native subject, vast differences in language, lifestyle, clothing—everything—reminded the ethnographer of the gulf between ethnographer and subject, and hence the possibility that the ethnographer did not understand what the subject was saying. In contrast, in ethnographies of present situations, the navigator is likely to understand everything the subject says, for the simple reason that they speak the same language (are indeed likely to share many aspects of their backgrounds). But perhaps such understanding is only superficial—it is difficult to tell. Thus one of the challenges of refunctioned ethnography (in this regard both like and unlike traditional ethnography) is the need to pay close attention to what the subject is saying or really trying to say.

*   *   *

Data (in the broadest sense, to include experience, impressions, testimony of various sorts and weights, and the like) gathered, the ethnographer moves to the third stage, pulling the material together so that it is in fact raw material for her project, writing a professionally respectable (in that sense, authoritative) text. Various ethnographic conversations are analyzed—what was actually learned here?—and then brought into conjunction with things learned elsewhere, that is, synthesized. This is not a trivial task. The material is usually disjointed, even contradictory. Oftentimes, the incoherence of the data is due to the fact that ethnographies of present situations are likely to be multisited. The point is to understand the situation, not the perspective of this or that individual. Situations happen among individuals (and institutions, laws, recent events, expectations—the list goes on). Thus contemporary ethnographies ordinarily will involve conversations with multiple subjects and in multiple sites, often facilitated and hence mediated by different liaisons.

In weaving these threads into a conceptual net, the ethnographer usually will make use of critical theory, journalism, and history. Depending on the project, of course, other disciplines, for example, accounting or computer science, may come into play. The double motion of analysis and synthesis, the give-and-take between processes of distillation (the important thing here was . . .) and recombination (taking this and that together, a relationship emerges in which . . .) is inevitably a double simplification, but it permits translation from the world, through which the ethnographer has navigated, to the texts. If all goes well, the text she ultimately produces will represent some situation in a way that makes it more understandable to her audience.

A word of caution is in order. The ethnographic text produced should reflect the situation in question, but it cannot be seen as a mechanical reproduction of the situtation, or still less, a mirror of it. In general, the ethnography's raw material was not previously available, but instead was the product of negotiation and conversation undertaken by the ethnographer. In important ways, the data cannot be reproduced. One might have a different conversation, later, even involving the same people, but that would be a different conversation, later. . . . Only this navigator, then, was in this position, from which she participated in, observed, analyzed, and reported upon what she saw, that is, the conversations in which she participated and indeed largely staged. Only this navigator could say, I was here in social space, at this juncture in various narratives. And most important, the material from various sites was synthesized by the ethnographer in her conceptualization of the space among her subjects, that is, the locus of social activity whose position is exclusively occupied by no actor, and for which no one person can speak, no single perspective suffices. Thus, rather than a description or representation in the ordinary sense, which is in principle replicable, the expressions of ethnography for present situations are *in principle* unique. What ethnography for present situations offers is the chance to gain a deep understanding of some situation within the world, but that understanding is also inescapably personal and must be read as such.

To summarize the foregoing: ethnography for present situations is accomplished through six basic activities: negotiation, evocation, attention, analysis, synthesis, and expression.

CHAPTER TEN

Why?

For my friends Doug and George, there are obvious reasons to think about ethnography—the practice is arguably the core of their discipline, cultural anthropology. Now that the concept of culture does not make sense in the ways it once did, cultural anthropologists might want a theoretical articulation of (an idealized view of) contemporary practice; a programmatic view of how their own ethnography, and ethnography in general, should try to develop in order to be interesting and effective; a sense of how students are to be trained. For George in particular, who is sufficiently prominent and senior to play in disciplinary politics and who is committed to the work of those he has trained, the question of where the enterprise of cultural anthropology is going carries existential weight. Not that George is gloomy about the matter, and various things may happen, but he has after all devoted his professional life to the development of this complexity, this "humane inquiry," and so he cares.

For me, the question of "why concern myself with contemporary ethnography" is not so obvious. Indeed some of the reasons I find myself in this conversation have little to do with ethnography per se at all. Each in their own way, both Doug and George discovered and enthusiastically supported my own work during a period when, frankly, I needed to be discovered and supported, and I deeply appreciated any enthusiasm. And I have always found it wonderful simply to talk with other people about ideas that matter to them, though I have gotten less combative with age (and probably with success, fat and happy, that's me). Besides, I have learned a great deal about academic generosity from George and others I met through him (including Doug), at Rice and elsewhere. Those things said, my gratitude and sense of collegiality could neither have sustained the years I have spent talking and reading about ethnography, nor motivated me to write a book about our conversations.

There are of course substantive reasons I too care about cultural anthropology, albeit as an outsider. In part 3 of this book I maintain that ethnography can fulfill specific needs of academic intellectuals working at the present time. Refunctioned ethnography can produce insights that are simply implausible for other disciplines. As a result, ethnography may be of considerable benefit to the contemporary university in its effort to remain intellectually attractive. In part 4 below, I follow up on the suggestion made in part 1 that ethnography has potential to be useful for the conduct of politics, or more realistically, has the potential to provide a critical vantage point for intellectuals who perforce live under contemporary conditions and who do not wish to take the fundamentally irresponsible if ubiquitous tack of disavowing the institutions and polity that privilege them. That is, all I want to do is suggest how ethnography may help certain kinds of people, roughly speaking, intellectuals, to understand their worlds, reinvigorate their institutions, forgive themselves, and perhaps participate in politics. And give peace a chance.

Joking seriously, a substantial impediment to humane thought at the present time is the earnest quality of so much intellectual life. As in the last paragraph, books commonly are justified by vast promises to improve the world, or perhaps only one's own existence. While it is worth pondering why utopian design and self-help receive so much attention from my social class, and why these enterprises are undertaken in a voice of disingenuous rationalism, perhaps the greatest cause of the dreariness of contemporary thought lies in the very structure of the class. In an economy in which "knowledge workers" are paid so long as their demonstrable expertise is in demand, much of social discourse will take the form of rational argument. Through such argument, people will claim to be acting reasonably, because they have thought carefully about ideas that they have somehow established, often through education, which is a good thing because it helps us to know, and which only incidentally excludes people not similarly educated, that is, just happens to protect market share. It is difficult to conduct humane thought—to make connections—under such conditions.

In welcome contrast to much of the contemporary university, which increasingly resembles an especially competitive version of Weber's iron cage, or better, a landscape of fortified towns, ethnography affords the possibility of a certain aesthetic of lightness, accessibility, and even adventure that is very attractive. As a discipline cultural anthropology has little by way of intellectual apparatus, and much of what it does have can be learned "on the fly." To shift imagery, one might say, with Lévi-Strauss, that "[l]ike mathematics or music, anthropology is one of the few genuine vocations. One can discover it in oneself, even though one may have been taught nothing about it."

This is not to be antimethod or antipedagogy, in anthropology or elsewhere. Training clearly matters, in both music and mathematics, and with regard to pedagogy, throughout part 2 I suggest a way to teach people to conduct ethnographic conversations. I do mean to insist, in a tradition going back at least to Socrates, that teaching is a secondary activity, helpful, sometimes absolutely necessary, but not originary. The midwife is neither the mother nor the father. (But the modern university is obsessed with intellectual property, and few administrators want to learn that they hold at best a second mortgage on the truth.)

Among university disciplines, cultural anthropology is hardly defined as a discipline: its walls are badly guarded, and it is easy to enter. To claim to understand culture or the human or something so grandiose sounds implausible to many other people, who are human, trained in other disciplines, and may understand a thing or two themselves. The very breadth of cultural anthropology's traditional ambitions tends to undercut the proposition, usual in the university, that this discipline has a particular and exclusive form of knowledge that can only be approached by adepts who "understand the discipline." Anthropology's walls are too long and cannot be defended, and this is an advantage for anthropology at the present time. Far better to sally forth than starve to death or be overrun. (The Athenians abandoned their city and took to their ships.) Far better to do ethnographic research and learn about the world than to claim that knowledge is already secreted within the structure of the discipline. In contrast with economists or, I regret to admit, many lawyers, cultural anthropologists are open to new learning, from outside the borders, against the rules . . . and ethnography is how cultural anthropology acquires such knowledge.

A nomadic ethos is very special in an age of fortified hill towns. An aesthetic of traveling light, of resourcefulness, of employing people, scholars, and other materials found along the way, as they may be useful to the project (*bricolage*, one must say) still prevails in cultural anthropology, at least by comparison with its disciplinary siblings. Adventure, paradigmatically including travel, is an important corrective in today's knowledge economy because adventure entails a lack of commitment to one's own position. The traveler, by definition, leaves. The adventurer, by definition, puts something, even if only the comfort of his own position, at risk in order to seek something new. Money is spent to go on an expedition. If thought is obstructed at the present time by the fact that, for knowledge workers, expertise is a euphemism for a protected market and education is also a form of property, indeed their livelihood, then adventure may be a way to entice such privileged (rich) people to free themselves from the constraints of their position. Ethnography licenses people, especially students but others as well, to spend some of what they have in order to seek something new, that is, to explore what they do not understand and cannot defend (exclude others from). And if ethnography is a way to organize such adventures, then the discipline of cultural anthropology, less a castle than a camp, is a way to create an institutional space for the thinking and writing that adventure requires and occasions.

As a full professor (mistakes were made), I cannot help remarking that tenure might seem to be another way to encourage a more playful intellectual spirit, but by and large tenure does not appear to work that way. Perhaps by the time scholars have accomplished enough to be granted tenure, they tend to have forgotten how to play. Although who knows—the contemporary university without tenure might be even more dreary!

* * *

An ethnography of present situations might be especially welcome in my own field, law. For law, the problem is not just that area after area of legal discourse is essentially moribund, pettifogging, and generally not much fun. It may be dismaying mostly to law professors, but any number of practitioners, after describing something they regard as relatively interesting, will qualify themselves by saying, "It's still law, of course." And as a friendly anthropologist once asked me, quite disarmingly well into a good dinner, "But why would you think of law as an intellectual discipline?" What lawyers do is powerful, maybe, but isn't it a bit much that I ask it to sparkle, to be intellectually entertaining? My thought (hope?) is that ethnography can make law more human and more interesting.

Properly asking after and addressing the relationship between contemporary legal academics, who have existed in their present incarnation for only a few generations, and the university writ large or the laws, both of which are far older, would require another book. And perhaps entertainment is a bit much to ask, but the point I am trying to convey here is somewhat more modest. Law is a creature of the imaginary, and no discipline confronts and attempts to articulate the imaginary more directly than cultural anthropology. The adventuresome spirit required and promoted by the ethnographic enterprise, which in itself would be a welcome change of tone in the law schools, could help legal scholars better articulate their own commitments, help them know themselves, precisely because it confronts what lawyers suppress. Rephrased, lawyers need anthropology, not because the anthropologists know some critically important fact that lawyers do not, but as a license to speak freely.

A few words on why law is a creature of the imaginary might be helpful, especially to nonlawyers, who tend to have overly objective and factual conceptions of law. As Justice Holmes famously said, law is a matter of "felt necessities," the sense that some things are required of humans in order to be lawful. A similar notion underlies the international law doctrine of *opinio juris*, the idea that certain actions are performed in certain ways because such ways are believed to be legally required. Legal interpretation is, like the closely related enterprise of theology, a matter of understanding signs, meanings. The work of interpretation is done within armatures or frames that are embedded in the mind of the legal scholar and allow it to operate and that are difficult to perceive clearly. Ethnography can help clarify the frames employed by law—that is what it means to articulate the imaginary.

In law, however, squishy talk about the "imaginary" tends to be suppressed. This does not mean that law or legal scholars have no imagination. Indeed, the law has an incredibly rich and intricate imagination, built up over centuries and in some cases millennia, and many fantastic creatures found in the law are found nowhere else. When asked why this or that is required, however, lawyers and even law professors tend to answer with various forms of authority (statute, court decisions, fundamental rights, customary practice, scholarly opinion, reasoning from any of the above .. the list goes on). Such authority, however, in turn raises deeper questions—why this authority and not that one, what gives the "authority" its authoritative status, and the like. This regress grounds itself—like Kafka's image of the gatekeepers guarding ultimately unimaginable gatekeepers—in the depths of the imagination.

One can understand that judges, Wall Street lawyers, and other people important in various affairs would not want to indulge extended discussion of possible imaginations of the law, to say nothing of the uncertainty of it all—that would be no way to decide a case or close a deal. At least in principle, however, legal scholars, who are presumably leisured intellectuals, might seek to understand the legal mind, to plumb the depths of the law's (of their own) imaginations. Unfortunately, however, very little scholarship seriously engages the imaginative terrain on which so much of law happens.

Among the many reasons for the halting character of legal thought: contemporary legal scholarship in the United States remains entranced by advocacy and flatters itself that it makes a difference politically (see earlier comments regarding utopia and self-help). Legal academics also operate under complicated and awkward notions of both the substance and form of scholarship, that operate to ensure that little is read. Perhaps many important things are therefore missed, but what can be done? So much is published, almost all of it unpleasant to study. Scholars and indeed search committees now openly admit counting publications in lieu of reading them.

Legal scholarship tends to be far more concerned with the scholar's position in the legal academy than with either "the law on the books," as the old phrase has it, or with the world that the law is widely presumed to address. But the professional obsessions of the legal academy are understandable, not only for the reasons attributed to knowledge workers generally, but more specifically, because so much of the law is so boring that practitioners must be paid enormous amounts of money to suppress their mind's rebellion and "master" their subfields and the intricacies of their clients' problems. For those fortunate enough to be academics rather than practitioners, a small number of reasonably interesting, familiar, and easy to work upon questions define subdisciplines. The almost unimaginable amounts of published legal scholarship address these well-established questions and therefore fit squarely within subdisciplines, and in consequence are professionally respectable, even if almost completely redundant.

Might something more be imagined, at least for people who have already secured sinecures in the academy? Might the sense of adventure licensed by ethnography cause legal scholars to pursue their own assumptions and commitments, that is, pursue the Delphic injunction to know thyself and therewith begin philosophy? In the unlikely event that this were to happen, we might observe a period of real excitement in the legal academy, on a scale not seen since the 1930s, and perhaps not even then. While we have no Depression to spur thinking, there is more than enough for lawyers to consider these days. But within the legal academy, questions that should be very obvious in our society simply are not addressed by established professional discourses. The bankruptcy code is being used for an unannounced industrial policy, and securities law proceeds on inchoate conceptions of capitalism. Both public international law and antitrust (competition) should be more or less scrapped and begun anew. We have a woefully inadequate conception of bureaucracy, and consequently hardly any positive theory of regulation. Nor do we understand how executive power is extended or perhaps limited by bureaucracy (a question of constitutional significance at the moment). One could go on, detailing literatures that exist only in embryo if at all—but my point is that a sense of adventure about the imaginary is precisely what the legal academy needs, and what, at least in principle, a reconfigured ethnography might provide.

*   *   *

None of this means that ethnography is a universal solution, or that it has no problems of its own—the rest of this book articulates and preliminarily addresses some of those problems. Nor do I wish to exaggerate those characteristics of ethnography that, I will maintain, make the enterprise especially worthwhile in today's world. Those things said, however, ethnography has much to offer contemporary intellectual life, which part 2 has indirectly suggested in the course of describing a possible way of staging conversations in order to understand present situations. But it seems time to put cards on the table: I maintain that ethnography as here conceived can contribute to an intellectual life lived at the present time in three vital ways. Refunctioned ethnography is a way to think through higher education, politics, and philosophy today.

At least two difficulties confront anyone who seeks to obtain what we might call "higher" education: first, the plethora of knowledge and practices in the global morass; and, second, the disinclination to believe that any such knowledge or practice is, ipso facto, worthy of respect, the "suspicion of metanarratives," to repeat Lyotard's famous phrase. Economically viable command of some subspecialty goes without saying, simply because it is economically required for everyone, including the guy who fixes the photocopier, but simply knowing something other people do not hardly suffices for higher education, or for that matter, to qualify one as an intellectual. So what is worth knowing, if you are given the privilege of choosing? How is one to gain purchase in such a thicket? How to decide what to learn?

The answer refunctioned ethnography offers is essentially the same (non)answer that cultural anthropology has always offered—adventure. Adventure addresses two central problems attendant upon education in our time. First, with regard to the global morass, the ethnographer is invited to go out and find something she suspects might be worthwhile and design a research program that teaches her about it, until she has something worth saying publicly and being listened to. That is, ethnography invites its adepts to say that *this*—whatever *this* may be—should be considered, rather than consigned to the global informational morass and left unthought. *This* is worth our attention.

And what about the second difficulty confronting higher education, the suspicion of metanarratives? Why will the ethnographer take what she finds seriously? Because for the ethnographer as navigator, who was there, her narrative is not a metanarrative. What the navigator has learned is a part of her world. Indeed, if our navigator is a student, what she has learned through her ethnographic research is simultaneously how she has learned to think as an adult. She is the author of her own *Bildungsroman*. Or, to put the idea in French rather than German terms, the navigator, student or not, is given the incredible privilege of living out, to substantial degree, that nobleman Montaigne's idea of a life as an intentionally constructed narrative.

But the significance of ethnography—at least an idealized ethnography, in principle—extends far beyond the difficulties of getting a graduate education. Most contemporary education is about learning something that can be traded upon in the knowledge economy. Therefore, for all the blather about lifelong learning, our educational institutions powerfully inculcate an essentially static conception of knowledge as expertise, that is, property ("human capital"). Questions of certification are critical in the university and its progeny in public and private bureaucracies: who is authorized to speak, and on what? (Who holds title, and to what?) Those who are not authorized may be excluded as not understanding the discipline, that is, as trespassers. But ethnography begins from the assumption that one is not authorized within the world of a subject. Ethnographic knowledge reconstitutes itself with each project: in beginning a project, the ethnographer, like the novelist, abandons much of what he learned through the last project. Ethnography travels light, and in doing so, has the potential to offer not just a different perspective but also a different mode of intellectual life, even within the heart of the university, but more importantly, after the university days are over. And the contemporary university needs that critical perspective, needs to be reminded that the institution is not coterminous with the life of the mind.

Refunctioned ethnography has as much to offer thinking about ostensible politics as it does the slow politics of education. This is not entirely new, because anthropology traditionally has fostered a politics of critique. In seeking out foreign, strange, primitive ways of life, classical anthropology maintained that even the strange was deeply human, and perhaps could teach us the most about the range of what it meant to be human. Classical anthropology thus also taught that the human was very strange. Cognate dualisms suffuse the anthropological tradition. Insisting on the "scientific" study of other cultures—and particularly insisting on a general theory of culture—was bound to minimize the differences among people and cultures. (And even observed cultural differences often were felt to be lessening in the march of modernity). At the same time, insistence on the study of particular cultures, the publication of books and the creation of a discipline, was also insistence on the specificities of the culture in question. This culture was special, anything but normal, in the sense of already known in the metropole. And by extension, perhaps a given practice in the metropole was special, too? If the practice was special, a quirk of life in London or New York, then perhaps it could be changed? In its simultaneous if somewhat antithetical insistences on general humanity and cultural specificity, anthropology long has been a way to open intellectual terrain for social criticism, a way that was both sympathetic and reformist, to use an old-fashioned and probably irretrievable word, liberal.

Refunctioned ethnography continues to foster this liberal stance because it simultaneously acknowledges the humanity of its subjects while recognizing that their positions are quite specific. We all may be modern, but we are all uniquely located. One of the purposes of navigation is to find out where we are. And, at least in principle, we may move—another purpose of navigation is to find out where we are going. Thus the shift of anthropological attention from discrete and diverse cultures to diverse positions in a global context reproduces, in a different key, the context for what I have called the liberalism traditional among anthropologists. Refunctioned ethnography encourages a degree of sympathy and a degree of optimism that social change is possible.

However, refunctioned ethnography facilitates contemporary political thought in at least two additional, and perhaps more important, ways. First, as said above, ethnography can help to articulate the context in which politics takes place, the spaces in which the collective consciousness is formed, and makes up its mind. When did it become conceivable to remove this regime, even irresponsible not to? Who convinced everyone who mattered what was the right thing to do in this situation? Perhaps once upon a time (into the Kennedy administration, I think) it was possible to believe that different sorts of politics were done within the precincts of the various institutions established for the purpose, for example, that congressmen made up their minds to declare war. But in a time of political transformation and political celebrity, it becomes clear that the "social," largely defined by anonymous bureaucracy (who programs the teleprompter?) is the seedbed of the political, and questions of where and when the real work of politics is done, and by whom, become difficult to answer. As the foregoing section in this chapter tried to explain, as we come to perceive ourselves within our worlds, infinite variations on the Kafkaesque question, "What is the law?" become unavoidable. A function of ethnography is to structure such inquiries.

Second, refunctioned ethnography may foster a sense of responsibility. In insisting on the interconnectedness and the possibility of movement (that any boat may reach any other boat) refunctioned ethnography forces us to confront the possibility that our version of the modern is not the only possible modern. We are more than a little responsible for our contemporary. But to acknowledge any responsibly for the present situation, at least to some degree, is also to admit a degree of guilt. While political guilt, particularly in our culture, tends to invite bathos, seriously understanding that we are responsible might encourage the powers that be to ponder, with perhaps some sense of humility, whether they are exercising their powers in a worthy manner. At present, governments operate without substantial ideological opposition (and here we are living at the end of history), and therefore governments need to establish ways to criticize, even limit, themselves.

But perhaps the most interesting contribution of contemporary ethnography to intellectual life broadly understood is not to education or politics but to abstract thought itself, philosophy. Classical cultural anthropology oscillated from core to periphery and back, and in doing so, tended to destabilize conceptual categories. What counted as primitive? Or as modern? This inability to locate decisively, and so comfortably normalize, one's own conceptual categories produced the uncanny feel that marked ethnographic encounters, and therefore it made sense that cultural anthropology was important terrain for the postmodern turn. The ethnography for present situations articulated here takes this sense of the uncanny as its starting point—for contemporary ethnography, the question is not destabilizing inherited categories, but establishing what the operative categories are. Ethnography for present situations is essentially comic, trying to piece things together, as opposed to critical, trying to break things apart. Schiller, in his *Aesthetic Letters*, insists that philosophy springs from play–ethnography offers us a way to play, seriously, with the structures that we have just discovered in this new world. Refunctioned ethnography helps us to find places to begin thinking again, after the great transformation.

The possibility that ethnography can provide intellectual lives outside of anthropology with (1) a viable aesthetic of adventure; (2) a fairly disciplined preoccupation with the imaginary (that would otherwise be exiled to self-help or suppressed altogether); and (3) a sense of intellectual play in an age of intellectual property seems more than enough reason to try and reconstruct ethnography so that it addresses our worlds.

*   *   *

Part 2 has attempted to provide an image of ethnography for present situations to play against the traditional image represented by Malinowski, in which

> our ethnographer finds herself mystified by some aspect of her world;
>
> she reads and studies, alone and with others, to learn what she can to understand its contours;
>
> she enlists the help of others, liaisons, who might help her gain access to subjects who have something important to say;
>
> she engages in conversations, some long, many short, stretched out over weeks, months, or years. As she gains the confidence of her interlocutors, she learns their views of the world, of how they achieved their positions, of what they claim, hope for, and fear;
>
> she analyzes and then synthesizes what she has learned, charts the situation determined by these points, as a constellation is sketched by stars;
>
> she writes, as best she can, what she has learned; and just maybe
>
> she rediscovers (or never went through losing) academic life as the license to wonder; and it is even possible that
>
> she understands herself to be at home, or at least a comfortable wanderer, in her world.

PART III
In the University

The principle of Discipline (including Religion) is that '*there must be some rules.*' If you in-quire the reason, you will find that the object of rules is to relieve the younger men of the burdensome feeling of moral or religious obligation. If their energies are to be left unimpaired for the pursuit of athletics, it is clearly necessary to protect them against the weakness of their own characters. They must never be troubled with having to think whether this or that ought to be done or not; it should be settled by rules. — F. M. Cornford

CHAPTER ELEVEN

Rupture and Continuity

How might the conception of ethnographic work laid out in part 2 engage the academic discipline of cultural anthropology as it now exists?

What difference does this ethnography for present situations make for theory, for fieldwork, and for academic production?

How does such a refunctioned ethnography operate vis-à-vis other disciplines?

What sort of academic life is entailed by the ethnographic practice laid out in part 2?

Part 3 addresses such questions.

*　*　*

Understanding how the emergent ethnography of present situations engages cultural anthropology is difficult in part because the discipline does not now have a stable or cohesive view of what it is about, with which emergent practices might be contrasted. Rephrased, it is hard to articulate what is new if what is established is unclear. This problem is a consequence of the present state of intellectual discourse within the discipline, which is confused. This is historical happenstance; cultural anthropology has not always been such a cipher. Indeed, this book uses as a foil a stylized version (caricature?) of classical ethnography, evoked by reference to Malinowski. But Malinowski does not represent contemporary cultural anthropology, for the simple reason that he lived some time ago, and it would be wrong to understand the ethnography of present situations as a rebellion against him. On the contrary, our conversation has been concerned with conserving or even recovering the impulses, excitement, and to a large extent, the intellectual aesthetic of Malinowski and other old masters, albeit perforce in new circumstances.

Not that any simple return to the (idealized) tradition of cultural anthropology is possible or even desirable. As mentioned in part 1, the world has changed. More narrowly, during the 1980s the discipline of cultural anthropology went through a substantial rupture with its tradition. Because the rupture was in many ways successful, references to the "tradition" must be placed in quotation marks. The tradition has been problematized. At the same time, and as discussed below, because the rupture was in many ways partial, no comparatively authoritative new account of the discipline, no new paradigm, has arisen. It therefore would be mistaken to approach ethnography for present situations in the romantic terms of rebellion against a clearly established order (a preferred form of intellectual narrative) for the simple reason that no such order, no deeply felt and finely articulated consensus view, exists.

The rupture of the tradition of cultural anthropology preceded the development of ethnography for present situations; contemporary ethnography takes place in the glorious ruins of classical anthropology. As already suggested, ethnography for present situations presumes the classical tradition and indeed attempts to renew that tradition in a new key. At the same time, ethnography for present situations is acutely aware of ways in which the classical tradition is over, that is, it also presumes the rupture. Thus ethnography for present situations should be understood neither as an effort at revolution nor counterrevolution, but instead as a response to the conflict, not exactly a synthesis, more an intellectually belated answer to the question, what do we do afterward?

To which students, outsiders, and other neophytes are likely to ask, "After what, precisely? What is this 'rupture' within the 'classical tradition' of cultural anthropology?" Proper answers to such impertinent questions would require an intellectual history, which this book is not, and that anyhow should be written by someone whose view is less beholden to a central participant than mine is to George. Fellow nonveterans may need something of a substantive explanation, however, so let me offer my understanding of what happened, of the terms in which the academic tradition of cultural anthropology was attacked and of course defended, and so provide some intellectual context for the problems, internal to the discipline of cultural anthropology, for which this ethnography for present situations aspires to be an answer. I understand that this is a fool's errand. Veterans of those years will almost inevitably tell me I have it all wrong.

They are heartily invited to commit, in print, to their own simple and accessible intellectual histories of folks still living, and face the ensuing music. For now, I can insist that roughly the following narrative, whatever the extent of its truth, has formed the background to our conversations.

The rupture in cultural anthropology can be fairly if perhaps simplistically characterized as a series of battles around four major (and interrelated) lines of attack on the discipline's traditional self-understanding. During the 1980s, critics of cultural anthropology charged, from within anthropology, that the discipline in which they had been trained and as traditionally understood had the following serious shortcomings:

1. Cultural anthropology was insufficiently self-conscious of itself as a discipline.
2. Cultural anthropology made bogus claims to producing "objective" and hence "scientific" knowledge.
3. Cultural anthropology was colonial in attitude, and often profited from colonial power in fact.
4. Cultural anthropology denied its own writing and was therefore deeply hypocritical.

As anyone at all familiar with academic controversy would expect, discussion tended to turn from "certain intellectual problems in cultural anthropology" to "a critique of the work of the preceding generation of anthropologists," that is, to "trashing my life's work." Passions ran high.

Let us take these criticisms, which we may label "reflexivity," "epistemology," "politics," and "expression," in turn. The young lions—a list would only aggravate folks left off and perhaps some listed—argued, first, that anthropology was not sufficiently *reflexive*. Ethnographers were so eager to study wild people on islands that they tended to be unself-critical about their own enterprise. In their focus on the "native subject," cultural anthropologists tended to be rather thoughtless. Worse still, ethnographers treated their subjects, really interlocutors, as if they were not, like all humans, capable of self-reflection, were not self-conscious in their explanations of their culture to the ethnographer. To use an anachronistic image, traditional ethnography was charged with treating people who collaborated in doing the work of ethnography as if they were mere databases in which cultures could be somehow "looked up."

Reading the classics of anthropology, this criticism often seems somewhat off-the-mark, but one can see how it ("you are thoughtless") could be hard to deny. Surely the great ethnographers were acutely sensitive to their own intellectual apparatus and indeed to that of their interlocutors. But among the classic writers, as with Freud, neither the urge to force often exquisite interpretive facility into the intellectual form of the natural sciences, nor the resulting deformations, can be denied. And in terms of understanding a discipline, the high-water marks are not always the best guide: a great deal of less than wonderful anthropology has always consisted of the rather thoughtless mechanical deployment of a conceptual toolkit upon the raw material provided by a member, assumed to be representative, of some exotic culture.

Were anthropologists to think hard about what they were doing, the young lions in the '80s maintained, they would cast their entire enterprise into substantial doubt. In particular, second and *epistemologically*, anthropologists who took a step back and examined their field would see that their claims to be doing "science" were strained at best. Within this epistemological argument were at least two broad strands. First, empirically, a host of counter-narratives emerged that flatly contradicted the received account of given cultures. Gentle islanders were discovered to be marauding killers and so forth. Thus, rather than elaborating an increasingly sophisticated, precise, and verifiable description of various cultures, and perhaps even a general theory of culture, anthropologists found themselves mapping out a field of arguments, disputes, and questions of interpretation regarding what they had been told. Rather than progressing, like chemistry, anthropology appeared to be bogging down, like literature. The second wing of the attack on cultural anthropology as science was that anthropology's claims to scientific objectivity were undercut by the contested nature of the discipline's categories. Indeed much of what came to be called poststructuralism (and postmodernism more generally) was an elaboration, and response, by Derrida and others, to the linguistic structuralism of anthropologist Claude Lévi-Strauss. Thus cultural anthropology was a primary site of the broad reevaluation of thought that marked the twentieth century, which is sometimes known as the turn to interpretation.

Third, *politically*, the ethnographic encounter was suspect. Consider the following pairs of concepts: modern/traditional; future/past; metropolitan/primitive (or exotic); white/brown; male/female; science/magic; insider/outsider; colonial/colonized; literate/illiterate . . . One could extend the list or reorder it in other suggestive ways, but in traditional ethnographies, the ethnographer occupied some or all of the first, clearly superior, positions, and the native subject occupied the second, clearly subordinate, positions. Ethnography thus conceptually reprised the structures of domination that characterized the nineteenth- and twentieth-century politics of France, Britain, and the United States, the nations in which the discipline was developed and flourished. To sharpen the critique, one might note any number of instances in which ethnography was permitted, facilitated, or at least protected by the real power of the capital—our young man from Paris is, after all, of the ruling class. And to sharpen the critique still further, if one looks at any number of ethnographies, for example, at Boas and the American West, the discipline has often been impelled, hurried, by a sense of impending loss—that soon, the native way of life will be no more, drowned by the modern. Indeed, while there are still cultures and places less than modern, our idea of the exotic is a pale shadow of its former self. The waning of the exotic, more importantly, of the discrete cultures that our young man found so exotic, was perhaps inevitable, but it was brought about in some part by anthropologists, who, like tourists, destroy the essence of what they had come to discover. Ethnography thus stood revealed as the handmaiden of the rapacious modernity against which it claimed to struggle.

Fourth, *expression*: after the fieldwork was done, our young man from Paris returned to Paris and fabricated a story which, like Dante's poem, proceeded on several levels at once. Ideally, the story told of the conception, development, progress, and successful completion of the young man's research. At the same time, the story recapitulated the young man's foreign adventures, preferably combined with the stories of the native culture, unerringly related by the native subject—that is what the notebooks were for—all the while integrating this particular adventure, in this specific culture, in the broader (academic) story of culture writ large, the story of mankind told by the faculty. The central expression of cultural anthropology—the dissertation into book representing the first fieldwork—was a highly contrived production, indeed something of a tall tale. But the discipline presented such productions unself-consciously as truthful representations, just the facts. The critics in the '80s charged that this presentation was implausible at best, hypocritical at worst—the emperor had no clothes, was in fact just a young traveler, trying to learn about other people, no more. Under such circumstances, cultural anthropology could not be at all certain that it represented other cultures precisely or even fairly, hence the "crisis of representation" that came to summarize the entire rupture.

What was the result of this crisis? To what extent did anthropology succeed in reinventing itself in the '80s? Strikingly similar things were said in the legal academy, many under the banner of "critical legal studies," and on balance, it seems that nothing clearly changed in the law as a result, and very little changed in the legal academy. In anthropology, however, all four major critiques were successful in important ways. Anthropologists today at least try to be more self-conscious, less certain of their results, more sensitive to their political situation, and perhaps overly obsessed with various mysteries of expression. That is, the rupture of the '80s succeeded in changing the virtues (the morality) of anthropological practice, and so *perhaps* the practice itself.

Now that the crisis of representation has also become part of the tradition, however, one has to admit the exaggeration in many of the arguments made in the '80s. Ethnographic fieldwork always involved conversations, indeed highly self-conscious conversations, rather than the cold objectification under clinical conditions implied by the criticism. So why the strong charges, the high voltage? The ubiquitous, indeed by now reflexive, references to Foucault's thought provide a small but I think symptomatic example of what happened within academic ethnographic discourse, and for that matter is still happening. Foucault echoes through the crisis of representation in good part because he was so adept at articulating a frightening version of what it is to be modern (*Frankenstein* for professors), a modernity that may be righteously opposed. It is tempting to ask whether such histories, which so well serve contemporary needs to establish a stance, are to be trusted as history, but the question misses the point. It would be foolish to understand such historical narratives as history per se. Instead, such narratives are foils against which contemporary intellectual stances (politics in the very loosest sense of public self-presentation) may be constructed, not unlike the bill of particulars in the Declaration of Independence. What was, and to some degree evidently still is, at stake for the participants in such ostensibly "historical" narratives is the understanding of what it is to do ethnography, and so cultural anthropology, and so what it is to be a certain kind of intellectual. For those involved, the stakes are existential (or, to use different language, about the belief system of a certain elite caste . . .).

* * *

So let us confront the disciplinary rupture, and especially its aftermath, as an existential matter, not merely how the "discipline" as an abstraction somewhat ethereally "is constructed" or "ought to progress," but instead as also practical questions of how some people are going to work, evaluate their work, and so understand themselves. So where are we now?

As an activity, and however politically incorrect it may have been from time to time, classical anthropology based upon ethnographic conversation was generally a worthwhile thing to do. Reporting on the languages, stories, beliefs, lifeways of a remote tribe added to the store of (Western) knowledge. For all the difficulties and complicities of intellectuals, surely knowing about other people is a fine thing? As this book has tried to convey, such positions are, like art done in another period, both respectable (of art, one might say even heroic or worshipful), and yet altogether impossible. That is what it means to have a "rupture"—in some significant ways, the tradition does not propagate. The line fails; the (doctor) fathers do not beget sons.

In academic circles, such questions are usually presented as arguments. A maybe powerful but deeply intuitive sense of what work is worth doing now is usually expressed as the logical result of critical analysis. One is likely to hear arguments that, while work remains to be done along traditional lines, it tells us little about the vast majority of people in most situations. Or rhetorical queries as to whether it is possible or desirable to make a valued restatement of what one now must hesitate to call the "native" point of view ("no," is the looked for answer). Or why bother with the cumbersome apparatus of anthropology if there is nothing to discover, if the "native" is operating in the domain of "the already known" (as Annelise Riles calls it)? Anyway, shouldn't the native be speaking for herself? Don't other people (journalists, politicians, even lawyers) speak for the native, that is, the special interest, at least as well as any anthropologist could? What does cultural anthropology have to offer here? One could go on, but the question is always, also, why live like this as opposed to doing something else, maybe going to law school?

As now, such existential questions were presented during the rupture of the '80s in theoretical terms, as if they were to be resolved by clever debate. (This was more than a little ironic, as much of the critical theory deployed in the '80s insisted on the indeterminacy of debate, but for a while, arguments about the inadequacy of argument seemed worth having.) As a result, at least superficially, anthropology became much more "theoretical," that is, scholarship began to refer to and otherwise incorporate a rather diffuse yet socially recursive body of works that were collectively referred to as "theory," as the word is used, for example, in the journal *Theory, Culture and Society*. The "theory" at issue in this usage tends to be written by people trained in philosophy or literature, though often written in a historical/narrative mode, tends to be Continental (especially French), and tends, perhaps most importantly, to be skeptical of claims made by academics or others to produce "truth," "science," or other "metanarratives." Familiar names influential in anthropology included Bourdieu, Deleuze, Derrida, Foucault, and Lyotard. Like many other disciplines in the U.S. academy, anthropology became "postmodern" (deliciously, almost everyone involved soon disavowed anything like postmodernism, but reenacting that comedy of manners would take us too far astray).

Within anthropology it was immediately recognized that the adoption of all this theory would pose problems, and what might be done with theory today is the subject of the next chapter. For now and more generally, the widespread adoption of theory, in this particular sense, had some importantly beneficial effects on the field as a whole. "Poststructural" theory disabused cultural anthropology of its urge to declare itself a natural science manqué. Indeed, the new theory subdued, without entirely displacing, the old theories that had been understood to be cultural anthropology, notably symbolic anthropology, structural linguistics, and the study of kinships. Thus, after the onslaught of the new theory, there was little or no theoretical subject matter that anthropology could claim for its very own vis-à-vis other disciplines. Various theories were employable by anthropologists, but no such theory was exclusive to anthropology, and therefore no theory characterized the discipline. Cultural anthropology was no longer defined in terms of a specific viewpoint on the world. Anthropology hollowed itself out.

Without an internal program or agenda of its own, anthropologists were more than happy to go along with the programs of others. Cultural anthropology began entering liaisons with and for that matter begetting any number of disciplines (or at least university departments and working groups of various sorts), ranging from area and cultural studies, history, law, literature, science studies, women's studies, and the old flame, sociology. The (predictable) political proclivities of anthropologists became more explicit, and efforts to harness anthropology to public service became commonplace. As a result of these engagements, all sorts of research projects became imaginable, and at least in principle, respectable enough. The conversations that comprise this book would not have arisen in the context of a cultural anthropology much more narrowly imagined.

As part 2 was intended to demonstrate, the absence of a substantive paradigm, heralded by the failure to define culture, need not be an obstacle or embarrassment but can instead be treated as an opportunity to construct an empty vessel, a ship that can be loaded with intellectual content depending on what is acquired on the voyage. So the question must be re-asked, assuming that the discipline of cultural anthropology as instantiated in U.S. universities and after the rupture of the '80s can respond to such a conception of ethnographic practice: does such an (academic) life provide an attractive way to live? Addressing that question requires some sense of what these existential questions, contested in such high-flying language, have come to mean in practice.

*   *   *

As with most narratives of social change, one might also tell a story of continuity. The philosophical arguments within cultural anthropology during the '80s did not change the fact that graduate students still need to get dissertations, and more generally, still need to be certified by their elders as "real" anthropologists. In order to be successful, students have to do what is recognized as good anthropological work, that is, they must acquire a strong basic education and background, they must do fine field-work, and they must write up what they have learned in intelligent and professional fashion. (In the business of teaching the young, a very conservative and generally commendable impulse often decisively comes to the fore.) More specifically, students since the rupture have been taught the critiques made during the '80s, but also have been taught much of what the critiques were said to have discredited or otherwise displaced. Anthropology simply redefined itself as a bigger tent. (The same thing happened in law schools.) Although the range of subjects acceptable for doing dissertations broadened, the dissertation still required fieldwork. In general, fieldwork continued to be understood in essentially the same fashion as it long had been, with multiple tacit expectations about the pace of research, the advisability of living abroad, the authority of having "been there," and other markers of "good work." Even though expectations for the content and style of the dissertation, the significance of the dissertation for a student's subsequent career, and the audience for fieldwork all shifted somewhat, the form and presumptions of the dissertation shifted hardly at all.

The sort of partial or schizophrenic modernization that has prevailed within anthropology since the '80s has produced a few oddities. Any number of the dissertations and/or books that have been published in recent years about very contemporary aspects of the global context are situated in fieldwork done in highly out-of-the way places, the love children of vibrant professional expectations that ethnography be done on the periphery and of mounting interest in using ethnography to study the present dispensation. Similarly, with the dearth of truly exotic subjects, there has been a noticeable tendency to exoticize the unfortunate, to engage in what might polemically be called moral Orientalism as an approach to contemporary life. (Of course, to make matters complicated, sometimes it is important to study victims—but that was also true of the Orient.) To sum up and exaggerate for emphasis: while the rupture of the '80s transformed the way the discipline articulates itself and even the subjects that it considers "in bounds," training and thus practice has proceeded, to a surprising extent, much as before.

But perhaps this is not so surprising. Intellectual history is always also the history of intellectuals, as my friend Jack Schlegel is wont to insist. If the young lions of the '80s seemed to disagree profoundly with their elders, there was also prosaic but existential agreement, namely, the young lions all became professors. Consequently and problematically, the critiques of the '80s were profoundly academic critiques. (One of the functions of this little book is to put the institutional context of cultural anthropology, the university, and so indirectly the enterprise of cultural anthropology, under some pressure—a little more reflexivity would be healthy.) Cultural anthropology has proven so resilient to what would seem to be devastating philosophical critique in part because the critiques were made by professors, who had every intention of being professors in the morning. (The legal academy in which I was trained was also enamored of "radical" yet professorial critique, but the institution of the legal academy was never truly on the table, and hence the critique was always, in some pejorative sense, academic, that is, learned but not serious. Even so, it made for shouting matches and ugly tenure fights.)

The problem that concerns me here is *not* whether an institutionalized intelligentsia, the vanguard of the proletariat, somehow failed in their bid to become heroes of the revolution (odd that one can joke about such horrors). Instead, I wish to pursue the idea that commitment to the university, as the context of thought, is not unproblematic for thought itself. Cultural anthropologists ought to be sensitive to the constraints of the social, including their own context. The decision to understand anthropology, even after the rupture, through the discipline of the academy, entails a commitment to a particular institution, with its own specific limitations. The academic context of cultural anthropology has consequences, not all of them benign, for the conduct of anthropology as a professional discourse, and more important for my purposes, for the significance of anthropological thought to other intellectuals. Indeed some of these limitations, for example, the strange relationships the university has to contemporary politics, should be of considerable concern to many anthropologists.

The young lions of the '80s critiques, who came of age during the '70s, lived through a time of substantial expansion in the university system in the United States, to some extent driven by the selective service system (graduate study was widely considered preferable to combat in Vietnam), but to greater extent driven by the shifting, and increasing, role that higher education has played in the construction of the U.S. economy. At the same time, the long generation of professors formed by the grand politics of midcentury, and even more by the postwar intellectual milieu that now seems impossibly attractive, the golden age connoted by the phrase "New York intellectuals," was beginning to turn over the reins of academic leadership. Serious anthropology students had good demographic reasons for their tacit assumptions that they would become college or university teachers. They wrote and otherwise performed for an audience of academics, and perhaps this gave them the confidence to be a bit outrageous, the academic version of the high-spiritedness that many people in the generation of '68 believed was revolutionary.

While becoming a professor remains the most obvious and a very prestigious career for an anthropology student, many students cannot get jobs. Anthropology (like any of the traditional professions, theology, law, and medicine) cannot understand its pedagogy exclusively in terms of the production of scholars for the simple reason that too many people study anthropology who will never be anthropology professors. If fieldwork is the first great site of potential change within contemporary cultural anthropology and a primary concern of this book, then the development of jobs and audiences for anthropology outside the university is the second. In particular, as anthropology develops functions and audiences more or less outside academic circulation (although few places in the contemporary bureaucratic meritocracy are entirely removed from graduate education; everybody goes to school), we can expect to see anthropologists begin to imagine their discourses vis-à-vis broader publics. Indeed, some such imagination is entailed in contemporary notions of public anthropology as a form of advocacy and, more broadly, seems to be required if anthropologists hope to participate in politics in any critical way.

What effect such developments might have on the training of anthropologists and particularly on the form in which ethnographic research is expressed, for consumption by nonacademic audiences, remains to be seen. It is worth considering, however, the extent to which the intellectual excitements of the '80s in anthropology were compromised by their context of reception in the university. In contrast, it might be hoped that this time around, intellectual purpose and social context might reinforce each other so that the need to refunction ethnography to address current questions at the heart of global society will be encouraged by the development of publics for anthropology outside of anthropology departments. It seems time for even professors to adopt an intellectual stance that, while perhaps quite respectful toward the university, is relatively untethered by it, much as a traveling lawyer might regard his hotel.

CHAPTER TWELVE

Theory

Like Gaul, the practice of cultural anthropology may be divided into three parts: (1) the tradition, especially as taught, that forms the intellectual context from which fieldwork is begun; (2) the ethnographic encounter, that is, the intentional staging of conversations in order to articulate the situation under investigation (or traditionally, the culture); and (3) writing that is imagined to contribute to the academic field itself, bringing things full circle. The student encounters these three parts ("theory," "fieldwork," and "writing") in roughly this chronological order—learning theory precedes fieldwork, which, once completed, is written up in the dissertation/first book. Once her student days are done, an ethnographer is likely to be working in two or even three parts of the field simultaneously—relearning or contesting the field; doing research; and trying to write—but a certain logical sequence continues to prevail, at least for the next three chapters.

The preceding chapter sought to relate the emergent ethnography for present situations laid out in part 2 to the academic discipline of cultural anthropology as it exists mostly in the United States in the early twenty-first century. The possibilities for ethnography in which we are interested are not sketched on a blank slate. Cultural anthropology, like any discipline, has a history, and as with any discipline, the history is usually presented in propositional form, ideological (even philosophical) move and countermove in some grand argument over whether the discipline ought to proceed in one direction or another. As chapter 11 demonstrated in passing, such discussions are very meta-, and tend to be expressed as a sort of intellectual narrative, or as a terribly abstract yet normative argument, "Ethnography should . . ." But abstract argument is not enough. As an emergent practice, the efforts to deploy ethnography to navigate the contemporary must, at some point, engage the traditional and embedded professional understandings of the purposes and significances of the discipline of cultural anthropology.

Another way to approach the problem of context, then, as suggested in the last chapter, is to engage neither the intellectual history of contemporary cultural anthropology nor its normative/ideological imagination of itself, but instead ask, how does ethnography, as refunctioned to ask after present situations, change the academic practice of cultural anthropology? If we take the three parts of Gaul, the activities of theory, fieldwork, and writing, then we might ask, how does the different stance urged in this book affect the role of those enterprises within "cultural anthropology?" I hope to suggest that if we are serious about refunctioning ethnography to confront present situations in the world, we will find not only a new world out there, but that neither "theory," "fieldwork," nor "writing" will mean the same things back home, within those special social environments known as anthropology faculties.

*   *   *

How does critical theory, as it now exists within the academic practice of cultural anthropology, relate to the ethnographic (and hence not simply theoretical) interrogation of the contemporary? Does critical theory help or obstruct our ability to do ethnographic research into the situations in which we find ourselves?

At one level, critical theory is integral to contemporary cultural anthropology. As discussed in chapter 11, the integration of critical theory into anthropology had far-reaching consequences for the discipline's construction of itself and, specifically, made possible the radical "emptying" of cultural anthropology presumed by understanding ethnography as a process of learning through social navigation. This account of the role of theory, however, is essentially negative. Critical theory opened up intellectual space and thereby made conversations such as this one possible, made it possible for us to think about how ethnography might address present situations. But once the space is cleared, what functions does, or might, critical theory serve within anthropology?

In hindsight, much of the relatively recent introduction of what is now orthodox critical theory into academic anthropology seems essentially tactical, a way of changing the terms of discourse to the advantage of those who sought to criticize the regnant practices in the discipline. When introduced as part of the rupture of the '80s, "theory" had the advantage of being impeccably intellectual, obsessed with questions of culture, interpretation, hierarchy, and the like. Theory was played on much the same field as traditional anthropology, and in many cases, for example, Bourdieu and even Derrida, drew from some of the same deep sources as the orthodoxy in U.S. anthropology, notably the French social and anthropological tradition stretching back to Durkheim—thus the relevance of "theory" could not be denied. Still, it was an Oedipal tactical move. The sons proposed a game they knew the fathers would not be comfortable playing.

Many things seemed to have been hoped by this tactic. In the nature of hope, the precise character of these objectives was vague, even inchoate, but some idea of an anthropology more open to the subject, a more collaborative, even inclusive, practice, and of course the end of anthropology's truck with colonial and other forms of domination, including those strictures imposed by an overly logocentric approach to intellectual life—something like that. As often happens with tactics, however, readings in critical theory gradually lost their character as a means of articulating specific arguments, and sometimes even advancing thought, and became part of ordinary practice. Readings in critical theory coalesced into a canon, reified for almost all students and the majority of professors, and endlessly reproduced in footnotes in the contemporary professional literature.

It is trivially amusing in the unkind way that academics laugh at one another that many self-proclaimed progressive intellectuals who strenuously objected to various traditional canons have participated in the construction of a new canon. Nor is my point that this canon, too, needs to be abolished, so that each student can find his or her own way. Canons serve their (essentially conservative) purpose of structuring an educational program. It is ridiculous to talk about being educated into a group without some shared materials; the absence of assigned reading lists does not freethinkers make. Nor am I arguing, at least here, that some other canon would be much better—at least for purposes of discussion I am willing to assume that a serviceable canon can be constructed out of critical theory pretty much as it now stands, with of course the addition of a few books written by me and my friends.

The serious disappointment, however, is that critical theory, writing that was intended to and that did provoke new and exciting thought in cultural anthropology and elsewhere in the university, now hardly seems to do anything of the kind. There has always been bad philosophy, and perhaps nothing is quite so fresh once it becomes required reading, but still, one may be disappointed. It is now annoyingly clear that simply requiring anthropologists to have read certain theoretical critiques grounded in philosophy, literature, history hardly makes students (and in due course, teachers) philosophical or gives them literary sensitivity or the ability to form historical judgments. On the contrary, canonical readings are often cited to "answer" questions at hand, thereby terminating thought. Critical theory as now institutionalized thus often fosters, or at least camouflages a lack of critical acuity and certainly stands in for earning one's ideas. (Here again, much the same thing happened in certain precincts of academic law.)

The prevalence of critical theory in lieu of critical thought is unfortunate rather than necessary or even foreseeable. Ironically enough, "poststructural" critical theory now serves to provide conceptual analogues to the essentialist limitations that poststructuralists often criticize in the work of prior generations. And the prevalence of this laziness in cultural anthropology is rather surprising, because laziness is hardly a characteristic weakness of the anthropological tradition. Travel, the learning of languages, and the sheer bother of fieldwork—usually, anthropologists have earned what they know. If anything, navigators are even more constrained to work hard, because ethnography for present situations, as described at length in part 2, is conceived as a vessel that only acquires content through the doing of the ethnographic work. In light of the diligence that characterizes fieldwork, that so much anthropology should have fallen so hard for theoretical citation in lieu of theoretical work is, well, disappointing. Cultural anthropology should be theoretically informed but not theoretically determined, as Annelise Riles felicitously put it. In contrast, a canon of critical works deployed mechanistically ("as Foucault has demonstrated") in the conception or synthesis of the fieldwork tends to preclude learning from the world or even learning from Foucault in serious fashion.

Critical theory does more than seduce folks who are understandably enough lazy or just desire certainty. More subtly but if anything even more problematically, critical theory seduces those who would be righteous by encouraging certain sorts of critical or progressive political "engagement" and in doing so mightily encourages ethnographers to adopt adversarial stances that tend to get in the way of doing an ethnography of present situations, with its reliance on collaborative subjects, which is in turn dependent on the existence of a rapport. Critical thought—and especially French thought in the humanities and the social sciences—traditionally has held itself out to be a political, moral, and literally existential activity.

This, indeed, is much of its attraction. The critical thinker is not merely a thinker: he is a political actor, waging resistance, furthering the interests of the proletariat, hastening the end of colonialism, or somehow otherwise progressive, that is, righteous. The righteousness of such thought, by now strongly implied by the word *critique*, lies in its opposition to the status quo, its adversarial stance. All of this may sound very old-fashioned, and it is, but how much "theory" today unself-consciously adopts such an adversarial stance?

A refunctioned ethnography, if it is to be serious about understanding emergent worlds whose goods and evils cannot yet be ascertained, often must withhold judgment. Contemporary ethnographers really should, as Freud famously said of cigars, consider the possibility that sometimes writing a paper is just writing a paper, that politics in any specific and serious sense is often in tension with anthropological work. Let me be clear. My objection here is rather purely intellectual, and intellectual in ways suggested by this book thus far. So I am not making the political point that while the posture of "engagement" is almost always earnest (which is why it is attractive despite being tiresome to others), it should very rarely be considered serious on its own terms, for the simple reason that academic intellectuals rarely affect much. Nor need we tarry over the extent to which adopting a stance, being engaged, remains a civic duty in these late days of republican virtue or at least remains central to forming an adequate persona. Nor am I going to argue to my fellow intellectuals, many of whom have so little else, that politics makes for inadequate therapy and paltry religion. I too have spent most of my life being politically engaged, and there is no need for cruelty. But while politics, psychology, or religion may impel us to relate our own thought to our political lives (or cause us to try and divorce the two), my point is rather different. What concerns me here is the fact that understanding critique as opposition, or in its more etiolated form, as the moral hygiene of the estranged intellectual, not only distances that intellectual from the world under analysis but also condemns the world and valorizes the intellectual. I cannot see well; I do not like; I am correct—it is possible to learn under these conditions, but highly unlikely. So insofar as we are concerned with coming to understand a world, an obvious place to start thinking would be by acknowledging our position within that world and beginning to navigate accordingly. Not only is the navigator epistemologically forced to acknowledge her position in the world she seeks to study, she must—at least imaginatively and conversationally—seek to enter that world subjectively. Navigation is not drifting. In becoming, in thought and word, if perhaps not in act or true belief, complicitous in the world, she must collaborate—a word now routinely used to describe the relationship between ethnographer and subject.

"Collaboration" is an unsettling word that unavoidably recalls Vichy France and the ideal of resistance as an intellectual and political act (or claim to fame—opinions vary) exemplified by Sartre. Surely resistance must be better than collaboration? More precisely, whatever the practical and intellectual shortcomings of the understanding of intellectual life entailed in "critical theory," surely the possibility of distance, intellectual autonomy, critical analysis, and even moral condemnation must be preserved? Quite apart from dramatic talk of Vichy France, isn't it important for anthropologists and critically minded academics generally to preserve some objectivity, some of what Bordieu called the scholastic stance toward social life? My criticisms of the use of theory in the academy—that it excuses laziness and fosters righteousness and hence misunderstanding—must go too far?

Indeed. What I have been valorizing as a way forward for ethnography may seem perilously close to arguing that the ethnographer should simply concern herself with the subject of the day, thereby giving up the distinction between ethnographer and subject, and for that matter, giving up any claim that the practice of ethnography makes a distinctive contribution to human understanding. From this perspective, the now common insistence on the objective significance of critical theory ("as Deleuze has demonstrated") or the exercise of moral approbation or blame licensed by critical theory ("and now, a reading of 9/11") are worthwhile if often clumsy efforts to preserve a scholarly stance. Critical theory stands in for the no longer tenable distinction between modern and primitive: it keeps us (ethnographers and their intellectual audiences) separate from them (subjects, to be analyzed).

*   *   *

Both the criticism and defense of the current practice of critical theory have some force. How are cultural anthropologists to avoid both the Scylla of preaching from a distant islet and the Charybdis of being sucked in by the powerful contemporary discourses that are so fascinating, thereby abandoning critical distance altogether? One place to start would be to find a new role for "critical theory" in cultural anthropology, and particularly in the design of ethnographic research. The contemporary understanding of "critical theory" is characteristic of our intellectual milieu but is not necessary, as any postmodernist should readily admit. Perhaps critical theory can be renovated to produce a different practice of critique, one that provides insights that would be more useful in the study of present situations?

To pursue this thought polemically for the sake of clarity and fun: work in the humane sciences in which "critical theory" has had the most influence tends to vacillate between an "objective" mode, an authoritative and institutionalized representation of reality (the method, canon, and the rest of the scholarly apparatus), and a "normative" mode, a more or less explicit subjectivity, which, once authorized, acknowledges few restraints (herein various utopian designs mostly recognizable as projects done on the political left). Rephrased, debased critical theory vacillates between pandering to the lazy and to the righteous. Many disciplines, for example, law, require that work make claims in both senses of the word, both objectively and normatively. Adepts are rewarded professionally in the discipline for the perceived strength of their claims, that is, the extent to which the adept reaffirms the discipline's picture of the world and cheers/boos appropriately.

Socially and institutionally, this structure seems quite stable. Perhaps the intense subjectivity of the adversarial stance adopted by the academic classes serves as a kind of safety valve or compensation for the frustrations of life in various circumstances—café society essentially helpless before the Nazis; the frustration of being very intelligent but not much more; and for our purposes, the frustrations of trying to think in the pigeon cote of the contemporary bureaucratic university ("My subspecialty may be painfully boring, but at least I'm very moral"). If the university demands that its faculty bureaucratize large portions of their lives, then elaborate charades of "political engagement" may provide the appearance and perhaps even a sense of having an authentic persona, of being more than just another rent-a-brain. For one in this position, sympathetic efforts to understand the position of the interlocutor are at best a waste of time and at worst collaborations with evil. The point is to demonstrate the existence of one's own personality through the intensity of one's political engagement, which almost always is opposition. The point of "critical theory" is to "trash" other positions. (This language was actually used in law schools back in the halcyon '80s.)

What tends to be lost in this bifurcated universe is the middle ground of situated judgment, where strong claims are less likely. Situated judgment, of course, is rather literally what a refunctioned ethnography should be trying to foster—the question is, what is the situation of the navigator? And here an ethnography of present situations that takes its lack of content seriously has much to offer. The ethnographer has no "native" position of her own to fall back upon—there is only a sketchy tradition, some influential writings, an aesthetic, and an attitude. Especially insofar as the navigator defines her project through the process of multisited collaborations, the structure under analysis emerges through engagement with the world. More than merely the navigator's judgment upon her object of study, situated judgment is required in order to negotiate the project itself.

I do not mean to suggest we throw out Foucault. What has now become the canon of critical thinking remains important, in moderation and especially for students, because it teaches two things. First, critical theory teaches how to understand ordinary life in terms of larger meanings. Oftentimes the larger meanings are inflated or simply wrong, but such misdirections can be corrected. What is vital is that students learn to look at facts and wonder about, eventually see, patterns. This is not obvious to the children of phantasmagoria, as Benjamin might have put it. Second, and related to the first, it is important to know how to take distance—a degree of distance is part of analysis. It is even important to know how to oppose, when circumstances warrant. To say that opposition is profoundly limiting as an a priori intellectual stance does not mean that opposition, based upon powerful critique, is not often necessary. And critical theory can help teach opposition—but only if one learns how to criticize, not just read about it. (Reading philosophy is not necessarily philosophical.)

To be situated is not to give up on criticism. The anxiety that I've attributed to Bourdieu, that collaboration is inevitably a process of cooption and, ultimately, a loss of identity, is easily overdone. Business people make judgments about their coworkers; professors make judgments about colleagues; doctors make judgments about other doctors . . . Such situated judgments can be made because the critic understands not just the matter being assessed but also the context in which that assessment takes place. Whether in business, the academy, or a profession, context is established not vis-à-vis a single point but in a space defined by many points. For refunctioned ethnography, the lesson is clear: fostering situated judgment grows out of multisited learning. Indeed, multisited learning—designing a multisited research program, analyzing one's disparate findings, and expressing something—will require at least some level of critical theory. The navigator must plan her project, and such plans are drawn up (inevitably altered with experience) through a critical abstraction, a theory. Thus ethnography is not merely the beneficiary of critical theory, it is an occasion for doing it.

This idea of a middle space that serves as the occasion and the ground for speculative thought is not an entirely new idea for philosophy—it was a similar middle space that the philological tradition sought to inhabit. An ethnography for present situations is constructed as a process or stance in which the ethnographer is flexible, willing to learn, and if not empty, certainly open to constructing a project around the world discovered. At the same time, in planning the project and confronting its results, including the arcane and quotidian things encountered along the way, the ethnographer attempts to ask what this means, abstracts, and considers how further plans are affected. The practice of ethnography demands, if not formal philosophy, at least social criticism, and provides the circumstances to earn one's theory. In this fashion, a revitalized ethnography can help avoid the reification of critique within the institutional structures of the university, and thereby can go a long way toward revitalizing critical theory—philosophy—within the space of our bureaucratic university.

CHAPTER THIRTEEN

Fieldwork

How, if at all, would the ethnography of present situations urged here affect the profession's understanding of what it is to do fieldwork? The question is rather fraught for professional anthropologists (in contrast, I find it merely interesting) because, everyone seems to agree, fieldwork is vital to cultural anthropology. Even though it is not clear how to evaluate fieldwork or even exactly what counts as "fieldwork" these days, the history, tradition, practice, and hope for what may be learned in the field powerfully sharpens, perhaps even defines, the enterprise of cultural anthropology writ large. Academics across the university read and write, but fieldwork is the distinct activity of cultural anthropology, the way the discipline does its own work.

At present, however, the professional imagination of fieldwork is workable but oddly unsatisfying. While the contemporary anthropological imagination has traveled some distance away from fieldwork as the scene of encounter with a foreign culture, no similarly sharply imagined conception of the enterprise has emerged to take its place. During the rupture of the '80s, the classical image of fieldwork—the young man sitting across a table from a village elder in the middle of a clearing in some jungle—was subjected to a critique of power. At the political level, the classical image smacked too much of the colonial situation. At the personal level on which fieldwork is done, the traditional approach seemed to treat the "ethnographic subject" far too much like an object, either for scientific inquiry or for romantic appropriation. To put the point strongly, ethnographers came to see fieldwork as a human inquiry that should be conducted humanely. At roughly the same time, cultural anthropology's increasing and entirely appropriate interest in modernity required the development of new ways of going about fieldwork and, in particular, who should be ethnographic subjects. Thus how ethnography was done, and with whom, seemed to be shifting in tandem away from the classical encounter. But shifting toward what? While within cultural anthropology it has become understood that ethnography is no longer structured in the old-fashioned way and often-times will not concern itself with traditional subjects, no new imagination of what ethnography now is has emerged with the evocative power of the classical image of the encounter with the native. This situation is of some consequence both to cultural anthropologists and to anthropology's other publics.

One purpose of this book is to suggest that "navigation" can serve as the central dramaturgical trope for an ethnography for present situations, and part 2 outlined how such a conception of doing ethnography today might play itself out in the field. However, before considering the con-sequences within the university ecosystem of taking "navigation" as the constitutive image of ethnographic work, it must be admitted that the old imagination of fieldwork remains serviceable enough for some purposes. Anthropology's two most important external publics, the humanities and, these days, large institutions that seek to use anthropology to understand their own "cultures," have no obvious need to reconceptualize fieldwork and, hence anthropology. The old conception works well enough for the humanities, who have since at least the structuralism of the '60s used cul-tural anthropology's broad conceptual grammars and wealth of particu-lar stories to make "critical" moves in academic politics and in society at large. It is easy enough to use anthropology to suggest that the arrange-ments of this culture are really just examples of (broad structure), and that in other cultures (example conveniently provided by some ethnographer), things are done differently. Therefore we might do things differently here. More recently, cultural anthropology and fieldwork have been important contexts for considering the importance of narratives, the power of repre-sentations in advertising, politics, and media generally, the formation of identities and social meaning, and so forth—the familiar bundle of "mod-ern" concerns. But this is not all that new: contestation of such categories, with the attendant hopes and anxieties, have been part of the critical edge that cultural anthropology has displayed since its beginnings, as a reading of Mauss criticizing the suppositions of economists suggests.

Similarly, the corporations, governmental organs, and other institutions that form one of the largest and most interesting audiences for contempo-rary ethnographic work are also quite content with the classical imagina-tion of fieldwork. After all, such institutions seek an outsider's opinion, and under the classical understanding of fieldwork, the subject was a worthy subject precisely because he represented a strange culture. And it is more than a little flattering to be treated as exotic and so worthy of intellectual attention. To his neighbors, Bob is an affluent drone who does something quite specific within the new economy, something quite boring to understand in any detail. In this regard, Bob is just like everyone else in his neighborhood. But to his ethnographer, Bob's job has mysterious, perhaps even somewhat sinister, meaning in its play across the globe, which is somewhat gratifying to all concerned.

The fact that outside audiences (and sources of patronage) for ethnography tend to accept the classical imagination of fieldwork places ethnographers in the position of sailing under somewhat false pretenses. More kindly, cultural anthropology is in a highly professional time, that is, the gap between the professional and the lay understandings of the enterprise is relatively broad. Contemporary anthropologists know that what they are said to do is not what they actually do, that their own real questions are quite different . . . but since real anthropologists understand, among themselves, how and why the public image is wrong, who really cares? Lawyers rarely work like their portrayals in media or even in the political imaginations of liberal law professors, but so what?

One problem with such polite worldliness, with allowing others to understand ethnography in classical terms that the profession no longer espouses, arises in education. The lack of a clear and public presentation of how fieldwork works nowadays means that students often begin studying cultural anthropology with very little idea of what they are undertaking—they in effect join a discipline that no longer exists. In the course of their education, students are gradually disabused of their preconceptions of how fieldwork works and, consequently, what the practice of anthropology entails. While refining a student's understanding of how to work is part and parcel of any professional education, bait-and-switch is something else entirely. (Such misunderstanding is the cause of much bitterness among lawyers, many of whom went to law school thinking they were going to balm social wounds, ensure international peace, preserve nature . . .)

Nor is the old imagination so easily outgrown. The classical understanding of what it is to do fieldwork constrains the design of projects, and ultimately constrains thinking, in ways that are difficult (and would be unkind!) to articulate in particular cases. But surely many studies of present situations, done with a modestly updated version of the classical conceptual machinery ("globalization among the ___"), suggest that old categories dominate thought long after they have been officially discarded. In the late nineteenth century, after the English legal system had been reformed to replace specific writs with general causes of action, the great scholar Maitland pointed out that the old writs "rule us from their graves," that is, it was simply difficult to think English law in other ways. More recently, the constraints imposed by "outmoded" patterns of thought are familiar in many postmodern and otherwise loudly progressive contexts, in which forms that are proclaimed to be inadequate, discredited, or over nonetheless must be used because no substitutes have been discovered or developed. The lesson would seem to be that discrediting is not enough. One must replace.

And even in decline, the classical imagination limits the critical (and ultimately political) potential of contemporary ethnography. While cultural anthropology always had a critical edge, from the classical perspective, the politics was always indirect. Cultural anthropology was always, after all, about *other* cultures. Ethnography of present situations, in contrast, confronts *this* culture. Any critical insight generated by an ethnography of the contemporary is already about us and, in that sense, already a political intervention, even if perhaps a noninstrumental one (we may observe without proposing). From this perspective, to imagine contemporary cultural anthropology as a transposition of the classical tradition (in which the victim substitutes for the exotic, and so forth), is to blunt the critical edge that contemporary ethnography can offer.

*   *   *

Cultural anthropology, at least insofar as it wants to confront present situations, is at something of a crossroads. It can muddle onward without a strong image of what constitutes doing ethnographic work. Outsiders will assume that cultural anthropology is what it has long been. Insiders will know better but in rather inarticulate, or at least undertheorized, ways. Alternatively, as briefly discussed in chapter 2, cultural anthropology can transpose the geometry of the encounter with the native of a foreign culture onto an engagement with, even advocacy of, the position of the marginalized victim of global modernity. Or cultural anthropology can openly adopt a new, considerably more open-ended structure of fieldwork (as described in part 2), and deal with the consequences. But what are the consequences, for the academic ethnographer, of refunctioning fieldwork? What does working through an ethnography of present situations—as opposed to classical ethnography—mean for the work lives of academics?

Compare the situation of the navigator of the contemporary with that of Malinowski, the paradigmatic young ethnographer on the beach of the South Seas island. The navigator is herself at sea, attempting to decipher the meaning of what she sees. Her perspective shifts as she moves. Many of the things she sees also move. The navigator plots and logs her voyage, recording encounters along the way, but no single encounter serves as a destination, that is, the report of an encounter does not constitute the study. The ethnographer is one who learns how to find her way among the swirling crosscurrents of contemporary social knowledge, exchange, life, and describe her particular journey to those of us who have not traveled that route. It is her journey.

In contrast, the classical encounter was at a fixed place. The places, the cultures, and the subjects awaited discovery and description. The difficulties confronting the ethnographer included getting there, and then understanding what he saw in this place that was so strange, and then being able to relate what he had learned to those who had not really traveled. The authority of the ethnographer derived from having "been there," and therefore being able to provide, in Geertz's famous phrase, a "thick" description of what the place was like, to outsiders who had never or only superficially been, perhaps as tourists.

One key to the abiding interest in the traditional ethnographic encounter is the pattern of contrasts between motion and standing still. The classical ethnographer voyaged, and so moved, to where the subject waited. The ethnographer was from a "progressive" modern society that imagined itself to be moving forward; the subject was from a traditional society that had existed for a long time and so was stationary. At another level, however, the ethnographer was from a society that, while progressive, saw itself as essentially modern (and understood modernity in transhistorical fashion). The subject, in contrast, represented a culture, and moderns believed that cultures disappear. Rephrased, the scientist's ways of knowing claimed atemporality, even while the subject's ways of knowing were seen to be disappearing, lending urgency to the ethnographic enterprise. Thus, at this register, the positions within the scene of encounter that were understood to move or to be still were reversed. The motionless native proved evanescent and thus precious and sad; the traveling modern proved to represent the atemporal future, if sorrowfully.

These patterns of motion and stillness are altogether different within ethnography for present situations. The navigator of the contemporary may or may not physically travel, but whatever travel she embarks upon will not bring her to someplace out of her own society. She may be shocked, but it won't be "culture shock" for the simple reason that the topic was always already her own culture, albeit perhaps aspects and parts of the culture that she had no prior way of understanding. Our navigator charts her voyage through crosscurrents, and currents shift, that is, contemporary ethnography is unlikely to understand its learning in atemporal fashion. Nor is our navigator in a position to assume that her society is progressive— she is a navigator of the contemporary, not necessarily the modern in any normative sense of the word. Many bad things are happening now and are intrinsic to who we are. It has become clear that "modern" is a very big word indeed, encompassing many possibilities—fieldwork should not be expected to generate data that can support claims to transhistorical knowledge, much less to aim time's arrow. The navigator becomes adroit, worldly, a skillful operator in a shifting environment.

What does this mean for the professional life of the academic cultural anthropologist? Classical cultural anthropology had tragic undertones: the story of sympathetic people caught up in inexorable historical processes, their doom. In contrast, ethnography for present situations is novelistic: the story of the ethnographer's finding her way in the world. Like novels, archetypically the *Bildungsroman*, ethnographies turn on the development of individual character, how the ethnographer learns and so changes her view of things and, ultimately, herself.

For present purposes, the difference between the tragedy and the novel marks a different attitude toward education (and hence the educational institution, the university, with its disciplines). In the classical paradigm, the ethnographer was a scientist, that is, a master and a professional. Education was necessary in order to become such a person; education was a stage en route to the point of the enterprise, science (which will fail). In contrast, in ethnography for present situations, education is not a stage. The ethnographic enterprise is, instead, structured as a process of education. The ethnographer may improve, but like journalism or writing novels, each project starts all over, and when it is done, it sheds little or no direct light upon the next effort. Classical anthropology aspired to be cumulative, but contemporary ethnography acknowledges it is amateurish, always beginning anew, simply because the questions are interesting. Neither education nor literature stops. There is something incomplete, even willfully immature, about ethnography for present situations.

Understanding ethnographic fieldwork and hence cultural anthropology as a process of education, resulting in a performance and requiring a set of skills, means that education cannot be understood as merely or even primarily the inculcation of some body of anthropological knowledge. Like ethnography, fieldwork is a discipline in the sense of a way, an aptitude, or readiness. To make the problem concrete: because the ethnographer conceives ethnography as a process of education, planning her fieldwork is a very critical step for a navigator. "Design" implies perhaps too much precision, that things can work precisely as intended, which would presume that the bounds of the research are fixed (which, in the best of contemporary ethnographies, they generally are not). Plans must organize efforts and focus energies, but at the same time, plans must be held open to take advantage of the opportune and the serendipitous and to cope with unforeseen setbacks. Thus what contemporary ethnography requires is a combination of knowledge and ignorance, a more or less skillful putting oneself in a position for things to happen. The project should be well planned, but the ethnographer should be willing to change plans as appropriate. The ethnographer must be casually prepared, focused yet flexible—the stance is contradictory. So the question is, how well does the ethnographer manage such tensions, make such choices? As one site leads to another, as the ethnography begins to weave a fabric of connections, the problem of judgment—is this likely to lead to something valuable for this project ?—compounds. The navigator must put herself into circulation, into the crosscurrents, indeed like the Argonauts who Malinowski studied, and find her way the best she can.

Ethnographic projects are also temporally open-ended, indeterminate. Sometimes this will be obvious in a practical sense: a given ethnography, of any number of situations presently critical, will not be completed within the span of time afforded. All concerned will come to realize that more time was needed to do the job. However vaguely imagined the "job" and hence "completion" might be, one can often tell when it is not finished. In many challenging projects, ethnographers are lucky to grasp an inkling of the reflexive modernity of their subjects. It is a great deal more to ask that the ethnographer understand the social currents in which their subjects swim. It is one thing to study, for example, corporate lawyers. It is another thing to understand how a reputation is made or how a practice declines. More deeply, however, the problem is not practical and occasional but fundamental and unavoidable: the question will always be, when has she learned enough?

Ethnographic projects thus recapitulate, at a deeper level no doubt, the problems they were begun in order to address. One is never "finished" learning, for example, about this or that financial market. Connections, once perceived, lead to further connections. But of course, something similar might be said of the imagination of classical cultural anthropology, too. Certainly one was never "finished" learning about this or that traditional culture. Yet there is something different about present situations, in which the cultural context cannot be presumed or maybe even well learned but is often continuously redefined so that the bounds of social space, the categories through which the project is conceived, must be articulated even while they are studied. The puzzles facing ethnographers as they confront present situations are but sharply drawn instances of the general problem of education itself in a society in which information is presumed to be available and the disciplines are best understood to be conveniences. The ethnographer, like all writers, must find a place where stopping makes sense. Thus fieldwork—and hence ethnographic inquiry and ultimately the discipline of cultural anthropology itself—are disciplined in the same open-ended, inchoate, yet powerful way that texts are disciplined by the process of writing. Writing culture indeed.

CHAPTER FOURTEEN

Writing

So where does the writer stop? Most simply, how much fieldwork is enough to sustain a good text? The last chapter argued that ethnography for present situations is informed, disciplined, by an aesthetic of production—ethnographic fieldwork is used to produce something, usually a text, and conversely, that text structures how the fieldwork is done, much as architecture is disciplined by the requirements of building, even if the building is often only notional. Similarly, theory can be organized by the design, planning and conduct of the fieldwork, that is, theory understood as social analysis is shaped by the social encountered, or to be encountered, in the field. Thus the requirements of a writing (the "graph" in "ethnography") inform fieldwork and theory and thus ethnography writ large. But this merely postpones the question: what kind of writing is an ethnography for present situations intended to produce?

The question used to be easy. Joining the ranks of academic anthropologists has long required the writing of a dissertation. Because we are all victims of our graduate education, the dissertation continues to mark anthropological writing years after it has been signed off on and shelved. The dissertation is if anything more central to education than it is to the production of scholarship: the tempo of graduate study is structured by the production of dissertations. Indeed many, perhaps most, students in anthropology learn how to write professionally by wrestling their dissertations to a draw. In short, anthropology, like most other disciplines (law is a notable exception), is everywhere marked by the centrality of the dissertation as a mode of production. (The legal academy is marked by the law review article, and implicitly, the appellate brief, as a mode of production.) Thus one answer, the traditional answer, would be that theoretical education and practical fieldwork are oriented toward, if not precisely structured by, the writing of the dissertation. Or, in the case of an established scholar writing an article or book (nobody who is not German should write two dissertations), respectable anthropological work demonstrates that the author could have produced a dissertation.

This answer, however, is inadequate for an ethnography for present situations. The dissertation made sense, perhaps, in the elite German university, in which individual scholars (revealingly still called Doctor-Fathers) trained their intellectual progeny. Even today, in the U.S. university, the dissertation ensures that novices do a great deal of reading, have the discipline to apply themselves over time, and acquire a modicum of the academic social graces. It is not an entirely unsuccessful mode of training, despite its infelicities. But insofar as an ethnography for present situations is felt to be necessary, the dissertation makes little sense, either for the training of the next generation of academics or, especially, for ethnography's other audiences. As a genre, the traditional dissertation entails assumptions about the academic enterprise that ethnography for present situations does not share. Fieldwork may be disciplined by writing, by the requirements of a text, as argued through this part 3, but the text thereby produced need not be a dissertation as traditionally understood. (Although for the foreseeable future, doctoral candidates will write lengthy texts called dissertations.)

Traditionally, dissertations were required to demonstrate basically two difficult things: first, that the candidate had mastered the pertinent literature, and second, that the dissertation made a plausible claim to contributing to that literature. If the dissertation met those basic requirements, the candidate was granted the authority to speak and write as an adept of the discipline. The traditional dissertation thus presumes a discrete body of knowledge that can be mastered (that the pertinent literature can be read), and that that body of knowledge progresses, is cumulative, (that a contribution can be made for which scholars thenceforth will be responsible). Such progress, in turn, rests upon the relative fixity of the concepts used to bound the discipline, frame questions, and mark advances.

In the context of ethnography for present situations, however, none of this makes too much sense. Mastery of what, precisely? The literature on central banking? On money? On economics? On the social scientific study of any of the above? Precisely because the navigator must learn about her situation (a situation likely to be attended by its own several literatures), one cannot determine, ex ante, what is to be read, although some knowledge of the history of anthropology ought to be required, as a matter of breeding. Nor is it clear the extent to which it makes sense to think of the work produced as a contribution to cultural anthropology in any but the most general sense. So an ethnography results in better understanding of central banking, to continue this example. This may be important and worth doing for all sorts of reasons, but it is unlikely to mean anything at all for ethnography considered, as here, as a mode of intellectual operation or a vessel. The field does not advance because the author understood something about the world. By the same token, a really wonderful expose of political corruption may be important for many reasons while doing nothing for the practice of journalism as such.

On the other hand, once the pretensions to mastery and progress are relaxed, then any good ethnography of a present situation is likely to appear to meet, albeit only superficially, the requirements traditional for the dissertation. Presuming a minimal degree of diligence, finding enough to read is not the issue. Present situations are intensely mediated; we are swimming in texts. An adequate immersion in such texts, as well as enough education to give one a critical apparatus, is likely to comprise an impressive reading list. Similarly, because ethnographies of present situations are in principle unique (each navigator makes her own trip, writes her own *Bildungsroman*), such ethnographies *all* make original contributions to the discourse. Thus the standards for cultural anthropology entailed in the traditional dissertation, mastery and progress, are impossible for the navigator to meet if rigorously applied and trivially satisfied if loosely applied. In short, and to repeat, the intellectual requirements of the traditional dissertation simply cannot serve as the regulative ideal of either theory or fieldwork, and so cannot discipline the refunctioned ethnography suggested by this book.

It might be nice if no discipline were necessary, if navigators could be completely free spirits. But this is not possible for complex reasons that can only be suggested here. Prosaically but importantly, most writers need communal support, institutional authority, in order to function at all. Matisse, for all his solitude, said the same thing about painters. Not the least important function of the university is to create positions due a degree of attention, thereby facilitating writing and so thought. Students are granted a reader, their teachers. This is even more true of post-docs, in whom faculties invested in. Collegiality (when found) helps ensure that even professors who are bad writers do not go completely unread. But while professional status assuages the anxiety of writing, the anxiety remains uncured (indeed incurable). Writing is a professionally constitutive act, and one had better write something respectable. One's career, and so one's self, are on the line, always. Is this guy brilliant, or somebody who ought to be under the highway overpass, rambling on about the radio implanted by the government? (No wonder academics write so predictably.)

But the psychological and social dynamics of writing and reading are only the more familiar half of the story; the more difficult problem is aesthetic and epistemological. The form of a text may be experienced as a requirement, an assignment, so that work is done according to rules imposed by someone else, according to a discipline. (The teacher demanded ___.) So, above, the dissertation was discussed in terms of what is expected of dissertations and what has been expected of dissertations since long before this candidate began his work. That said, all texts have forms and can only be understood in terms of some form. Insofar as ethnography issues in a writing (or other production), that writing will be received in terms of a structure, whether or not intended by the author. Ethnography cannot escape the expectations found in the structure of its expression. Thus, just as the traditional dissertation entailed a set of assumptions about the nature of scholarship, what we might broadly call an aesthetics, the expression of ethnography, however it may be refunctioned, necessarily embodies its own aesthetics.

One might hope that the navigator realizes this, understands that she is already beholden to what she has not yet produced, and from that position, she should self-consciously design her work. The navigator should understand her text to inform her ethnographic work, what she reads, how she designs her research, much as the planned or even only imagined production of a building informs architectural work. That is, a refunctioned ethnography should operationalize critical reflexivity so that self-consciousness is not merely deployed as a critique of texts and stances after the fact but is instead a part of the design and performance of anthropological work from the beginning. Such reflexivity is not unique to refunctioned ethnography, nor as complex as perhaps I've made it seem. Writers often get to work by thinking of an audience and finish by editing themselves. Schiller distinguished between naïve and sentimental poetry, between the unself-conscious expression of a talent and a performance that understood itself to be playing upon the feelings of its audience, including its author. Refunctioned ethnography should hope for sentimentality, in this sense, rather than naiveté.

Why? Most simply, it seems more intellectually respectable to be self-conscious of what one is doing. Cultural anthropology has on occasion (notably in the '80s) justly been accused of being insufficiently aware of how it operated. "Know thyself" is usually good advice for an intellectual. But caution is in order. If self-conscious writing seems, in the abstract, more respectable, experience demonstrates that a reflexive stance does not guarantee the quality of ethnographic writing. Indeed, reflexivity all too often licenses a baroque preciosity, a bathetic concern with my feelings, tiresome navel gazing. This is not accidental. "Know thyself" can all too easily be heard, especially in an insecure and therapeutic age, as "become self-centered, indulgent, snippy." To make matters worse, ethnography for present situations cannot avoid the central figure of the navigator. She plans and takes her trip, keeps her journal, and writes up the story of how she came to know something about the world. For an intellectual, however, coming to know is also coming to be (all entailed in the concept of *Bildung*), and so, as I have suggested already, the story is more or less explicitly a *Bildungsroman*, with the navigator as protagonist. And talking about oneself is difficult to do gracefully . . .

Given both the intellectual dangers inherent in reflexivity and the centrality of the navigator/author, considerable discipline is required in order to prevent egotism, or merely self-indulgence, from overwhelming the expression of an ethnography for present situations. (One might imagine a truly modest author. The truly modest, however, are likely to have difficulty sustaining the effort necessary to complete a substantial ethnographic project. Projects are completed by people who think both that their work is important and that they are very smart.) Ethnography for present situations is explicitly subjective and hence vulnerable to the flaws of its authors, always in danger of entering therapy, or less dramatically, writing indulgently.

The discipline required to rein in the self-indulgence of the navigator must be, in the first instance, essentially self-discipline, precisely because ethnography for present situations is structured as a vessel to be filled in the course of the ethnographic work and, therefore, depends on the personality of the navigator. Having asked the navigator to undertake a journey and report back, there is little principled authority within refunctioned ethnography for claiming, "You overplayed your role as protagonist." In contrast, traditional cultural anthropology, like most academic disciplines, defined itself in terms of a collective body of cumulative and objective knowledge, of the progress of the field, and such concepts can be used to ensure that the text and its author conform to professional standards. But like journalism, ethnography for present situations essentially relies on the situated and aesthetic judgment of its author, as well as its reader, to lend form to texts.

This is not to say that ethnography for present situations is merely subjective, journalistic, or even, to preempt polemic, therapeutic. As has already been admitted, self-indulgence is a real danger, so the question is how to avoid this danger. Fortunately, ethnography for present situations is informed by productive ideals quite apart from its normative aesthetic of disciplined reflexivity. Such ideals are to be found in the communication with audiences, and in the concern for the world that audiences want and indeed are often in a position to require.

Ethnography for present situations defines itself vis-à-vis audiences outside the department of anthropology, in addition to, not in lieu of, the traditional professional audience. The traditional audience, within anthropology departments, is not the only audience or even the paradigmatic or regulative audience. While the next generation of anthropologists needs to be trained and professors still need progeny, the context within which scholarship is traditionally done, the university, has been democratized. In anthropology as in other disciplines, hordes of students (in comparison with the nineteenth and most of the twentieth centuries) require teachers. As a result, more teaching jobs exist, but nonetheless, most graduate students will not in fact become professors. So if the first audience for ethnography of present situations is composed of professors and would-be professors, academic professionals, then a second audience might be students and other amateurs who think that anthropology is interesting. In this group we might also put folks from other disciplines, and even the rare but not quite extinct general reader.

There are other audiences. Some students will go on to work within anthropology but not in research universities. Members of this third audience may or may not call themselves anthropologists; they may or may not get another degree. They are likely to work in industry, for large charities, in government industries, and other organizations that are interested in their own "culture." This may sound esoteric, faddish at best, if one has an image of the anthropologist as university scholar firmly in mind. But in a world of human relations departments catering to the needs of vast institutions, concern for institutional culture is widespread, and so there is demand for ethnography. Such ethnographers may be thought of as practitioners; such organizations may be thought of as clients or even patrons, who comprise a fourth audience. Finally, while patronage tends to be organized by institutions (capable of writing checks), contemporary ethnography is often

conducted among various sites and subjects. Ideally, the folks whose connections are articulated through the ethnography, who find themselves in
relation to one another, constitute a somewhat distinct fifth audience, the
subjects. Thus ethnography for present situations addresses at least five
somewhat overlapping audiences: academic professionals; amateurs; practitioners; clients and patrons; and subjects.

The characteristics of the various ethnographic productions addressed
to these different audiences are negotiated, if often tacitly, with the audiences. So, for example, clients hire ethnographers because they believe
that the discipline has something to offer them. The task is the discovery/
application of particular, practical knowledge that is useful to people who
have other things to do today. Such a production (in the practice of law,
sometimes called a "deliverable") might be expected to look quite different from traditional academic writings.

Specifically, ethnography written for public or private sector, but nonacademic, clients often must respond to the quicker tempo, the lack of
time, in which such clients generally live. To be more concrete: productions for clients should be more accessible than traditional academic writing. Long texts should be summarized for people with relatively short
periods of focused attention to give to the matter. Presentations are likely
to be more visual, and less wordy, than is the norm for the academy. By
the same token, because clients tend to want to know about themselves
rather than the discipline or even the world in general, only matters of fairly
obvious direct relevance to the patron should be treated at any length. Bibliography, and indeed supporting material and even argument, should be
suppressed, perhaps included by reference or attachment. The author's understandable concern for his own intellectual position vis-à-vis the profession, revealed by arguments and discussions of "the relevant literature,"
also should be suppressed.

Ethnographic work done for a client generally responds to questions
asked by the client, questions that unsurprisingly often reflect problems
confronting the client. Such ethnography is commissioned in the hope that it
will provide or at least contribute to a solution. Presentations of such work,
therefore, are likely to be fairly practical and in that sense normative. The
anthropologist must be able to answer questions such as "What's the take-
away?" and "How might this insight be implemented" in clear and concrete
fashion. While the ethnographer is thus put into a normative position, the
production should be delivered in less strongly argued/more diplomatic fashion than is common in the academy, where arguments are generally made

with little regard to the difficulties of little matters like forming consensus, setting priorities, and implementation, that is, without regard to questions of management that figure only slightly in the academy, but that are vitally important to many clients. In short, production done for clients tends to be more businesslike than traditional academic productions.

Understanding ethnographic performance as a communication with an audience helps to keep the work focused on the questions that engendered it, or to put the matter negatively, the audience helps to keep the navigator from becoming overly focused on herself. Presumably, audiences are interested in aspects of the world discovered through the ethnographic journey rather than the ethnographer. While a few audiences, sometimes even teachers, might be interested in the navigator for her own sake, it is a simple matter to remind the navigator that being read by one's friends, parents, therapists, and other beholden folks is not enough to prove that one is a real writer. Writing and publishing are not the same things. Rephrased, once nominal membership in the discipline no longer entitles one to an audience of serious and critical readers, then the act of writing must discipline the enterprise.

The navigator and her audience(s), oftentimes including her subjects, are likely to have, or at least begin with, different interests. As already suggested, the temporality of ethnography is likely to be slower than the audience prefers. The navigator may experience her audience as impatient, as thinking "We get it," long before she believes they truly understand. This is a particular and common example of an essential creative tension, from which the navigator derives (or loses) her authority: the navigator claims to have something to tell. The expressions of ethnography for present situations are, as discussed above, fundamentally unique. The navigator demonstrates to her audience that not only are their interests different but also that she has something to say that the audience cannot articulate, something that is worthy of their attention. That is why they are the audience and why she performs—more generally, that is why ethnography is worth undertaking, even worth payment.

The relationships entailed in a performance are themselves bound in time, in the duration of the work, and therefore in substantive extent. Audiences lose interest or simply must move on to other business. Conversations run out; projects conclude. Such limitations inform and profoundly constrain the writing of texts, as the foregoing discussion of ethnographic presentations to institutional clients was intended to suggest. The disciplines imposed by audiences and subject matter on texts (and back of that, the

ways that producing a text inform research, writing, and thought) are familiar enough in the practice of law. Legal briefs, a letter to a client, and a
law review article are very different texts, written for different audiences,
and internally limited in different ways. But such texts are limited, structured by their occasion, audience, and subject. How much is enough must
be asked of every such text, but it is a matter of judgment, indeterminate
but not a difficult question in principle.

By the same token, the question with which this chapter began (if ethnography is defined as an empty vessel, then how do we judge [or plan]
ethnographic work?) is recurring, unanswerable in principle, and not particularly troublesome in practice. This practical question may be reasked in
judgmental form: how do we ensure that ethnographic work is sufficiently
rigorous? What about standards? Such questions seem daunting only if one
tacitly presumes that cultural anthropology is structured, as the discipline
long believed itself to be structured, as the construction of a specifically
ethnographic corpus, as a social science conceived in the fashion of the nineteenth and most of the twentieth centuries, on the ideological model of natural science. As a philosophical matter, few cultural anthropologists would
admit to such a view (we are all postmodern now), but when it comes to
understanding ethnography to be continually reconstructing itself, nerves
falter. This is unnecessary. As this book has tried to show, the practice of
ethnography provides more than enough discipline to constitute an intellectually respectable enterprise. Instead of somehow "updating" a model
it no longer seriously espouses, ethnography for present situations opera-
tionalizes, makes practical and internal, what was once offered as a critical
(meta-, external) insight: ethnography is a form of writing. As such, the
difficulty of communicating something significant about the world provides
more than enough discipline to make the enterprise rigorous, intellectually
respectable, and to hold an institutional space within the university, that is,
to constitute a discipline.

CHAPTER FIFTEEN

One Discipline among Others

Part 3 has sketched some of the consequences for the academic discipline of cultural anthropology of the ethnography for present situations described in part 2. Rephrased, part 3 has treated the professionalization of navigation. Thus chapter 11 described ethnography for present situations vis-à-vis the tradition of cultural anthropology in the United States, as partially renewed by the critiques of the '80s. Chapters 12–14 looked at some of the ways that such a refunctioned ethnography might prompt reevaluation of the key academic modes in which ethnographers work (theory, fieldwork, writing). This chapter examines how ethnography for present situations (having publicly bid adieu to Malinowski) might understand its role in the university and as one academic discipline among others. What specific intellectual contribution does cultural anthropology make? How does it justify its space within the institution of the university?

A caution: as important as they may be to academics (who are also bureaucrats), disciplines are intellectual conveniences, ways of dividing labor, and not very significant in and of themselves. Surely the sorts of phenomena that comprise present situations, for example, central banking, can and should be considered by many different disciplines, anthropologically, economically, historically, legally, politically, sociologically, and so forth. Indeed, one cannot pursue any of these modes of inquiry for very long without wandering into another mode. And it should be obvious that my own interests, reading, and conversations are hardly confined to the discipline in which I am titled.

But my cavalier attitude toward disciplines, too, can be overdone. As a bureaucratic matter, at least, disciplines are not dispensable. University central administrators need to believe they have filled the positions a serious school is expected to have. While we can and should laugh at this, insofar as we intend to use the bureaucratic machinery of the university to provide sinecures for thinkers, and for that matter to structure the training and sorting of the young, various disciplines (no doubt all centers of excellence) will have to be defined. From this perspective, the question is why should cultural anthropology, after Malinowski, be expected to have a place in the contemporary university? What does cultural anthropology offer? Can that same work be done by other disciplines, that is, is there an opportunity for efficiency here? And while it is fun and healthy to remind administrators that they are due precisely the respect given to functionaries, there is an intellectually interesting question here: where does ethnography for present situations, described as "a vessel" in part 2 and professionalized through the production of certain texts in part 3, see itself in the ecology of knowledge?

At least in principle, it is hardly necessary that there be a cadre of professional ethnographers who confront our various situations. One can imagine the reefs and shoals of contemporary society being charted by people without degrees in anthropology, indeed by people who are not academics at all. A professional memoir, often written by someone who has just left a position that affords a good vantage point, can convey precisely the sense of structure and interconnectedness that one would hope from an anthropological account. Journalists, especially those who work through interviews, often produce texts with a distinctly anthropological feel. Even lawyers, with their strong sense of structure, sometimes write in ways that smack of anthropology.

The lack of a professional academic monopoly on anthropology is not accidental. Anthropology has been an amateur pursuit for longer than it has been a university discipline (here in western New York, we remember Morgan among the Iroquois), and the university has never entirely displaced other sites for anthropological writing. Today, when the subjects of inquiry are present situations rather than exotic cultures, and work is often commissioned by nonacademic institutions, ethnographers increasingly may be found outside anthropology departments. Indeed, the key assumption of paraethnography is that something akin to the ethnographic is built into the structure of life in contemporary flows of knowledge. People know how to navigate the thickets of their worlds precisely because they have imagined and so behave along lines that the navigator seeks to articulate in the fashion most effective for her audience, whether in the anthropology department or elsewhere. Simply by virtue of being aware of the global (or at least breathtakingly vast) contemporary, we are all perforce ethnographers unto ourselves, naturally with varying degrees of analytic precision and expressive power.

If we are all in some sense ethnographers unto ourselves, then people who one might hope would become involved, as subjects, liaisons, or otherwise, may decline to participate. Such people may feel quite entitled to do their own anthropology informally, under the guise of understanding how their world works, of knowing the score. Such people are often more senior than their would-be ethnographers, and they already know what's what. Why does a senior scientist need a graduate student to tell him the meaning of his work or the social workings of his milieu? He does not. Thus, if we do not simply presume, as academics are wont to do, the context of the university (their own context) then it is not obvious that other sites of knowledge production will not generate the sorts of analyses that refunctioned ethnography seeks to provide—the would be-ethnographer may be bringing coal to Newcastle, providing an unnecessary service.

Against this it should be noted that recent years have seen the widespread emergence of corporate and other institutional patrons of ethnography. In hiring professional ethnographers, such patrons presume that ethnography has something special to offer. Some large concerns have even founded small anthropology departments. Perhaps this merely reflects bureaucracy's need for academic certification to justify hiring decisions; many managers have degrees from business schools. But perhaps the hiring of academically trained ethnographers rests to at least some extent on a substantive belief that the discipline teaches something distinctive and, perhaps even more to the point, that professional ethnographers in fact generate knowledge that would, as a practical matter, otherwise be unavailable.

There are at least four reasons for this belief that professional ethnographers are not superfluous for the study of present situations. First, as a practical matter, while a degree of the ethnographic sensibility is required for participation in modern thickets, many modern actors are not going to be in a position to do ethnographic writing in any proper sense. The occasional memoir may be very good, but far too often people will be too busy, will have difficulty abstracting, will write haltingly—ethnography will not get done. Thus, if ethnography for present situations is felt to be valuable enough to do often and well, the enterprise needs institutional support, which of course is a function of the university.

Second, as discussed in part 2, paraethnography relies upon more than the fact that contemporary actors need to construct their own maps. Subjects often address themselves to an interlocutor, real or imagined (the market, the national interest). The ethnographer, then, steps into a conversation that is already ongoing. The navigator tends to be welcomed even though she is unnecessary for the conversation, which began before her arrival, and will continue after she moves on . . . From the perspective of the subject, the navigator is not necessary for the articulation of the ethnographic, but in order to be an audience, to hear the production.

Third, the ethnographer, like the priest, lawyer, doctor, or most of all, analyst, approaches as an outsider. Admittedly this can be difficult if the ethnographer is within the same organization (a difficulty regularly faced by the in-house legal counsel of large corporations). As a professional, the ethnographer is in principle not personally interested, which is not to say indifferent. The ethnographer's interest is derived from sympathetic understanding. Moreover, the ethnographer often has some learning—she has a theory, and knowledge, if often only secondhand, of similar or different cases, and therefore, a degree of perspective. Here again the ethnographer resembles other professionals whose work also requires such understanding, backed by a claim of expertise.

As with other professions, the ethnographer is invited (and therefore socially licensed) to make inquiries that others would find awkward. Ethnographers often ask questions that in other contexts would seem simpleminded, or to call for useless generalization, or would simply be intrusive, even embarrassing. The ethnographic conversation often turns into a somewhat impolite uncovering of what is actually happening, a more or less illicit discourse. One must be careful not to overdo "illicit"—ethnography can be done about many things besides the sexual habits of the Trobrianders, or their modern-day analogues in the seamier reaches of contemporary culture. Ethnographies of many stunningly boring and public situations are highly worth doing (weapons procurement, accounting standards, and trade regulation spring to mind). That said, the public presentation of almost any situation is almost never the whole story of how things "really" work in that world. As an outsider, the anthropologist is a plausible audience for such stories. Indeed, like the journalist, the ethnographer encourages such stories. Again like the journalist, if perhaps to a lesser degree, the ethnographer is vulnerable to sensationalism, and to being led or otherwise manipulated.

Fourth, as an academic, however, the ethnographer is in a position to rearticulate such illicit discourses in polite and cognizable fashion. Ethnography thus gains something of the frisson of the great nineteenth-century critical traditions (Marx, Darwin, Freud). Speaking freely, expressing what is widely known but not widely acknowledged, is something that is politically and socially and sometimes even morally difficult for the insider to do. Even subjects who have left their positions may be unwilling to write what "really" happened, at least if they want to preserve connections that, oftentimes, developed over decades. In such instances the professional ethnographer provides encouragement and license for the articulation of the otherwise unmentionable.

To recapitulate: even in situations in which subjects can be expected to articulate their own situations, the navigator serves at least four functions. As a practical matter, she is more likely to get the work done, and with a breadth and depth for which very few subjects will have the resources. Second, she provides an audience, which, third, is outside the world of the subject. Fourth, she is capable of restating the truth, even fairly uncomfortable truths. At least in principle, navigators provide a way for inhabitants of present situations to reflect upon, and even talk about, their situations.

If (professional) ethnography for present situations may be usefully, if not absolutely, distinguished from the (ubiquitous) ethnographic thought done by subjects as a matter of their own psychic survival, how does ethnography as here refunctioned distinguish itself from other forms of inquiry into the contemporary? In particular, how does ethnography for present situations see itself as different from journalism? Part 2 defined ethnography for present situations as an enterprise whose substantive content was found, as an "empty vessel." Chapters 11–14 defined the professionalization of ethnography within academic cultural anthropology in terms of writing for audiences. But journalism also has no subject matter of its own, and journalism is similarly organized (disciplined, and even taught in universities) by its need to communicate the contemporary to fickle readers. So how is ethnography, as here conceived, different from journalism?

That journalism and cultural anthropology are cognate, indeed often competitive, enterprises cannot be denied. Journalism, for example, does a far better job of reporting on the emergence and importance of this or that corner of global society's mansion. No graduate student can compete with the *New York Times* magazine when it comes to sketching the significance—at least as the *Times* understands significance—of some social phenomena. Journalists can draw on a wealth of resources (teams of smart individuals, money, access, technical savvy) in order to have significant conversations with important people. In a world with good journalism, why is ethnography necessary? Even if we have bad journalism, why is ethnography, rather than the reform of journalistic practice, necessary?

Although perhaps not immediately obvious, journalism, even in the best of circumstances, functions under profound constraints. (Let us leave to one side problems with journalism that may be very real, such as political bias, economic corruption, or censorship, but which are contextual, extrinsic to the practice of journalism itself.) Simply put, journalism is about the news. Temporally, the news, by definition, is recent, hence "new." The articulation of journalistic significance is necessarily quick; the story must be filed before commercial interest wanes. Socially, the news must be news to someone, that is, journalism is informed by and devoted to an idea of newsworthiness. As has been remarked in a thousand ways, journalistic significance is a function of mass attention. Journalism pays excessive attention to the sensational and insufficient attention to matters that, while rather uninteresting, might be important to an informed politics. Journalism is structured, or at least incessantly tempted, by celebrity.

From this perspective, we can see that journalism and ethnography are inverse enterprises. If journalism is quick, ethnography is slow. Some of this slowness is practical. Conversations occur over months, even years, and are written over further years, often published in more than one context, for different audiences, depending on how matters unfold . . . Some of this slowness is biographical. As academics, ethnographers have time on their hands, often in marked contrast to their subjects, especially those who work in uncertain jobs. (Tenure does change one's perspective.) But the languor of ethnography is not merely circumstantial. As chapter 8 tried to suggest, ethnography for present situations thinks through the present in ongoing terms, as a continuation of the not yet past or as the stance from which the future is and will be awaited. This is not news. It is already here. It is how we in fact live now, even if we are not fully aware of it. It is emergent.

Journalism and ethnography take reciprocal approaches to society. If journalism is obsessed with what is celebrated, matters of broad public awareness (and if both journalism and most of their subjects are highly self-conscious), ethnography is concerned with the not yet entirely conscious, that which the public is not aware of and does not celebrate. Journalism announces a war, or at least its rumor, as a matter of national interest. Ethnography asks how war came to seem imperative to those who decide such things. Ethnography concerns itself with the uncanny structure of social life, the way things connect, which is almost always different from the way things are said to connect. As with temporality, the predilections for the uncanny for the less than public has very practical, circumstantial aspects.

Ethnographic conversations tend to be held privately, in closed settings. Biographically, ethnographers tend to be obscure, and it might be hoped that their questions are not those of *tout le monde*. Conversations with ethnographers may well be more than public posturing. Through such conversations (and here the association with Freud is unavoidable) the navigator seeks to uncover the structure of the social, to be able to articulate her situation in some way deeper and more true than the overly accessible, indeed imposing, surfaces of highly mediated and fundamentally untrustworthy public presentations.

The ethnographic sensibility is endemic to modern life (as is the journalistic sensibility, of course). In fact, the ethnographic sensibility might even be seen as the shadow of the journalistic sensibility. To rush is not to take one's time. To be shown something is not to be shown something else, perhaps more important. To be conscious of journalism as a story is to worry that one does not understand the backstory. Ethnography is not replaceable by journalism; ethnography is required by journalism.

While journalism, along with most other jobs, now has its place in the firmament of "higher" education, journalism is hardly a traditional discipline. If we were to compare ethnography for present situations with various traditional academic disciplines (meaning those which have been taught in the university since at least the beginning of the twentieth century), however, it would be easy enough to show how refunctioned ethnography was distinctly organized, asked different questions, and so discovered aspects of the world that would be implausible for the adepts of other disciplines. An ethnographer, an economist, and a lawyer in a central bank are unlikely to learn or think the same things, but it would be tiresome to generalize the argument, which would require defining and distinguishing each discipline separately. In light of the considerable superficial similarities between refunctioned ethnography and journalism, the fundamental differences between the enterprises should be enough to suggest that ethnography makes a unique contribution within the contemporary university.

PART IV

In the World

In the lives of emperors there is a moment which follows pride in the boundless extension of the territories we have conquered, and the melancholy and relief of knowing we shall soon give up any thought of knowing and understanding them. There is a sense of emptiness that comes over us at evening, with the odor of the elephants after the rain and the sandalwood ashes growing cold in the braziers, a dizziness that makes rivers and mountains tremble on the fallow curves of the planispheres where they are portrayed, and rolls up, one after the other, the dispatches announcing to us the collapse of the last enemy troops, from defeat to defeat, and flakes the wax of the seals of obscure kings who beseech our armies' protection, offering in exchange annual tributes of precious metals, tanned hides, and tortoise shell. It is the desperate moment when we discover that this empire, which had seemed to us the sum of all wonders, is an endless, formless ruin, that corruption's gangrene has spread too far to be healed by our scepter, that the triumph over enemy sovereigns has made us the heirs of their long undoing. Only in Marco Polo's accounts was Kublai Khan able to discern, through the walls and towers destined to crumble, the tracery of a pattern so subtle it could escape the termites' gnawing.
— *Italo Calvino*, Invisible Cities

CHAPTER SIXTEEN

The Intellectual's Situation

Whether or not the United States continues to project force on the current enormous scale, the empire that is crumbling for us is an empire of the spirit, the Enlightened modernity of which the United States has been such a complex and powerful expression. The United States, and indeed much that we recognize as "modern" will no doubt continue—the alternatives are too horrible to detain us long—but will not continue in the same way. We cannot live in the republic of Jefferson's dreams; the dreams themselves are fading. This should be cause for a wry smile.

If we understand globalization as a new form of political life, then we must expect it to have its own grammar, different from that of the state, the form of political life that has been somewhat supplanted. And since the public grammar of the state, at least in the most powerful and modern places, has been unabashedly rationalistic, even Enlightened, we must expect the new politics to have a different relationship to rationality. Therefore, the status of intellectuals—those who understand the social "critically," that is, in terms of their rationalizations, and who frequently believe themselves to be doing politics thereby—is different in the new politics.

The fact that the social position of intellectuals has changed is likely to be resisted or denied altogether for the sake of appearances or hope. There was a great deal of comfort, sometimes even religion, in the modern stance, in which individual morality, institutional operation, and history writ large were knit together by ideological labor. But perhaps transforming the world is not enough. We children of Robespierre the lawyer have done incalculable damage, and ideological thought rarely rises above the level of good advocacy. So the passing of our kind of intellectual is probably good for both our societies and our thinking.

Still, those of us trained in the ruins of the empire of light cannot view the transformation of our way of life without deep unease. Surely we must care about politics writ large. How else, if not politically, are we to confront our fears of wars, nature, and much else? And surely our effort to conduct such politics must be as thoughtful as possible? Indeed, thoughtful politics gave publicly presentable meaning to our institutions, most especially the university, and even lent a sense of purpose to the lives of many individuals who had little else.

Such anxieties, which have in our time so deeply wounded the professoriate, are all too easily overdone. To acknowledge limitations is not tantamount to surrendering to chaos. To abandon nationalistic rationalism as a presumption of political thought is hardly to espouse nihilistic civil war or even to require a certain cosmopolitan lack of patriotism. The challenge and the opportunity of the present time is to develop more humane, modest, and tenable ways to be thoughtful about our politics, our institutions, and the stances we adopt toward one another. Light-hearted conversation is a promising place to start.

CHAPTER SEVENTEEN

The Imaginary and the Political

L et us assume, in fine Enlightenment fashion and borrowing the language of Keynes, that we are ruled by ideas and very little else. Politics, then, must be about the battle of ideas. So it might seem that we have at last made the world safe for philosophy, indeed we have made a world in which philosophies rule, or at least struggle for power. This would be very silly, of course, although most contemporary journalism, almost all of legal scholarship, and a fair amount of "public" posturing in anthropology and elsewhere in the academy assumes that government flows from argument and superficially understands arguments at face value, as logical arrays of ideas. Against such facile constitutionalism, it is worth remembering that as Keynes spoke, the cold war was beginning, and ideas tended to become something more primitive, ideology. More deeply, Keynes spoke of the governance of ideas even as he was constructing integrated markets that would make the political expression of ideas, as well as republican virtues generally, far less relevant. Nor have contemporary social developments, notably the establishment of the administrative state and the so-called information economy, and the attendant professionalization of thought, been kind to the play of ideas. When everyone is an expert, ideas become property to be branded or at least hoarded. Indeed Keynes himself is no longer a plausible figure.

Whether or not this is the golden age of political thought, politics, however and by whomever conducted, is done in accordance with some set of beliefs held by the powerful, an imagination of what can and should be done. Alexander and others must believe that it would be a fine thing for the Macedonians to conquer the world, or else they would have never left their hills and pastures. Thus there is a sense, Enlightenment or no, in which all politics is intellectual politics. For Keynes, the pressing economic and so political questions (how did the Great Depression happen, if economies

settle upon efficient equilibria, and what can be done about it?) were essentially psychological questions: at what point did people lose confidence
in their markets, and what can be done to restore such confidence? Or we
might ask, with Krista Wolfe's Cassandra, when did the prewar begin—at
what point were we already on our way to war?

Even to begin thinking about such matters is difficult in part because it
is truly difficult to know anything about the vast contexts in which we do
politics. Even in the natural sciences, and even ignoring the possibility of
a paradigm shift, verities are not what they used to be. So, for example, in
recent years, scientists have "discovered" that the "rogue waves" up to 100
feet tall, which have been reported by any number of sailors and damaged
ships far above the waterline, are not only not mythical, they are fairly common, although one has yet to be seen on any campus with which I have been
associated. Sticking with a very common substance, the molecular structure
of liquid water may have been misrepresented and erroneously taught to
countless students for decades. That is, as of this writing, even scientists,
and certainly the rest of us, are aware of our uncertainty regarding something fundamental and seemingly quite knowable. And the computer chips
of the world will malfunction at the millennium, unless they do not. The
medical profession reverses its advice so regularly that one suspects organized deception ("policy"). Oil has been running out, over and over again
throughout my lifetime, without changing price (and probably someday it
will), but by then the climate will have changed, to something warmer no
doubt, unless . . . This was going to be a huge hurricane year due to some
ill-defined extent to ocean warming caused by global climate change. But
the hurricanes did not materialize, which of course does not mean that the
planet is not warming.

My point here is not radically skeptical, that the natural sciences have
failed or should be abandoned or anything of the sort. My point is only that
we media consumers know quite little about the objective circumstances of
a great many things we might care about, and might even attempt to affect
politically. The problems of what we, as engaged intellectuals, really know
worsen, of course, if we begin to ask questions about the complicated,
constructed, and historically ephemeral phenomena of social life, markets,
nations, currency and the like. And so the Soviet Union dissolves; the United
States is doomed by imperial overstretch until it becomes a hyperpower;
stock markets now and then "correct"; Iraq does or does not have weapons
of mass destruction, and its people will or will not revolt; fashions come and
go; an era of peace becomes an era of war; new technology will make every-

thing different without changing anything; the President is a mindless front, unless he is a malevolent ideological genius; red states and blue states . . .

Our awareness of the tentative state of our knowledge is likely to grow when we stop and think about the vast scope of our concerns. Empiricism is generally impossible; what most people mean by "empiricism" is the bandying of numbers. (As the Chicago economist Knight sarcastically put it: if you don't know what you're talking about, measure it anyway.) Few people have seen a rogue wave, and far fewer of them are research scientists. Even among research scientists, relatively few bother to examine water molecules. Everyone has their own fish to fry. It is a postmodern cliché to note that knowledge is socially constructed, mediated, and communicated, but the point here is far simpler: almost all knowledge, even that of concrete things, is at best secondhand. Outside of very narrow specialties, we are all in a position of knowing only what we read, and of course it would be foolish to put too much stock in that.

Although a few people have seen rogue waves, nobody has seen the Soviet Union, or globalization, or international law, or any number of other concepts we use to organize our worlds. Many such concepts are simply ethereal (money, property, law, confidence). Many such concepts happen at such vast scales that they cannot be experienced and hence must be discussed as abstractions, that is, taken on a degree of faith (China, the Arab world, technology). Such concepts are very real, collectively imagined, but also, by their nature, incredibly difficult to know. The media and the academy, for reasons of their own, tend to employ such abstractions as if their meaning were more or less self-evident. This creates a faux empiricism, an illusory sense of concreteness. Political discourse is largely the normative manipulation of such phantasmagoria.

Even when we perceive correctly, we are all too often unaware of the significance of things happening within our sight, not because they are obscure but because they are hard to think, usually because our conceptual language simply does not articulate the right questions very well. Jean Monet said that the European project would make war impossible between Germany and France. It occurred to very few people that he was in effect proposing to reinvent the nation, and therefore, much of how politics, and so social life, is done. During the 1970s, the United States shifted from defined benefit to defined contribution retirement plans, thereby restructuring not only retirement, but labor and the middle-class ethos of capitalism. Such things happened in very public ways but were at the time literally inscrutable, unseen.

Many people (and almost all intellectuals, except the ideologically convinced or otherwise obtuse) strongly suspect that the politics they are able to articulate—what we think we know—is not the real politics. Many of us fear we do not know the score and that what we do know is surreal, floating on top of the reality that matters. A common response to the sense that the contemporary is not what it seems to be, to the democratization of the surrealist sensibility, is conspiracy, even demonization, which preserves the modernist illusion that social life is the product of politics and that politics is intentional. Present situations are attributed to the Jewish lobby; the neocons; various speculative investors; the vast right-wing conspiracy; the Beltway consensus; the military industrial complex, especially Haliburton; the Illuminati (also known as the Carlyle Group); the WTO . . . all of which has the marvelous advantage of lending a facile rationality to contemporary history. Many people desire conspiracy as an antidote to the *mise-en-abyme* of their own ignorance, and hence tend to exaggerate how much of contemporary life can be explained by the machinations of shadowy characters or the covert agendas of public figures.

The psychological tendency, even subjective yearning, for conspiracy might be understood as a political expression of the loneliness (anomie) that seems so characteristic of contemporary life, so often lived in vast contexts. Other aspects of such politics without community would be the need for imaginative sympathy in lieu of shared experience and the construction of celebrities—the need for a political imagination does not disappear once the polis is no longer an option and community, human contact coterminous with political concern, is not possible.

(This yearning for politics lends a certain pathos to contemporary life, a pathos that for the navigator serves as an analogue to the doom of the native—it underlines the fragile humanity of the subject.)

But the fact that we may yearn for politics and that such yearning even may cause us to imagine conspiracies does not mean that conspiracies do not exist. Power and influence and even agency over events certainly exist, and sometimes old-fashioned conspiracies are possible even if hardly common and rarely successful (or so I have been led to believe!). As already suggested, however, conspiracy is a simplification, which presumes that politics can be known, is in fact known by the players. People who are not players may console themselves with the hope of becoming players, or at least "blame the government and shovel hot food down." But perhaps nobody knows, or knows enough. Perhaps even the conspirators do not know. There are so many secrets in contemporary life. Some are obvious: the military, intellectual property, and much of finance abound in secrets. And much is a condition of the existence of multiple expert cultures, each with its own awareness that important things, perhaps decisive things, are happening elsewhere. One might even go so far as to understand the contemporary condition of this elsewhere, that is, to see globalization as a despatialization of the conditions of culture, rather than (merely!) a deterritorialization of national politics. But how, then, does one do politics with elsewhere, attempt to influence conspiracies as yet unknown?

Perhaps this obsession with the conspiratorial is just another version of the thought, running through the great thinkers of European modernity, that alienation, the modern condition, leads to irrational political passion, so amply demonstrated by modern European history. The contemporary generates its own irrational, an irrationality that more naïve moderns (and much U.S. public discourse, even today) assume will be overcome by historical progress. But progress has been going on for some time now, the modern is pretty much everywhere triumphant, and craziness abounds.

If we wish to confront the surrealism of the contemporary politically, then ethnography has a great deal to offer. Ethnography reminds us that our "knowledge," and therefore social authorization (power) to take action, is formed within the flow among social institutions. Far more common than shadowy figures who can individually control events are the ghosts within our social mechanisms, the structures and effects conjured within bureaucratic life, market interaction, fashion, and the like. So the question becomes, what are the social spaces, the pathways, through which the imaginations that matter come to matter, and eventually come to be politically operative? A decision to go to war or to raise interest rates, for examples, cannot be formed in isolation. Ideas and people arise and work together. Ethnography can clarify and make explicit ways in which such social connections are formed, channels through which information flows and decisions are made, the structures, in short, through which politics actually is done.

The political purpose of refunctioned ethnography could be to provide some intellectual purchase on the imaginations that are only superficially expressed as rational arguments through which we orphans of the Enlightenment persist in pretending politics proceeds. This purpose may be divided into three basic activities: (1) mapping the political imagination, (2) reflection, and (3) intervention.

The first stage, mapping the imagination, is both important and difficult to achieve. Mapping is important because, once well articulated, an imagination of politics may be thought through, analyzed, that is, real political criticism becomes possible (if not necessarily more efficacious than art criticism). As part 2 above should have served to demonstrate, mapping the imagination is difficult. After a moment's reflection, however, the idea that our political imaginations may be somewhat inaccessible to us ought to be troubling. Since almost all political imaginations these days are presented in explicit and rational terms, that is, in "Enlightened" fashion, such imaginations are open to public engagement, rational critique, and quickly can be demonstrated to be right or wrong. Modern government is "transparent," is it not? Stated baldly in the abstract, this suggestion seems ridiculously naive. We all know that political speech has considerable spin. Rationalistic language serves many functions, but how often is it what it most plainly claims to be, an unself-conscious articulation of the stages of thought? In politics, almost never. The transparent is also invisible. The function of ethnography here is to map the terrain, record the grammar, of the politics in question, that is, to find out what people are really saying.

To make matters worse, speakers themselves often have only a hazy idea of what they are saying, hence the importance of the second stage, the patient and critical reflection that the contemporary university, for all its faults, affords. The world constructed by the subject may be importantly wrong (but will be presented in rational terms anyway). Sometime interlocutor Olivier Roy provides a neat example: in the Soviet era, committed Marxists carved up Central Asia into nationally organized "republics," which, when the Soviet Union dissolved, emerged as nation-states, despite the fact that Marxism was antagonistic to the idea of the state. However today's central Asia came about, it is clear enough that the real significance of the subject's work may be completely misunderstood and thus unintended by the subject. The entire Reagan administration (to say nothing of the current administration) seems to have functioned, and indeed made world history, on the basis of conflicts among breathtakingly audacious imaginations, which, of course, had their own logics. (One may remember the bizarre fantasies of missile defense mostly forgotten under the heading "Star Wars.") And what law professors do when writing articles, preach the plausibility of bureaucracy, is profoundly different than what they say they are doing, rationalizing politics. Appropriate political response will, of course, vary from case to case—but the progress afforded in principle by refunctioned ethnography lies in helping us all think more deeply about political imaginations, and hence politics, than is now prevalent.

From this perspective, views of the world and what is to be done within it turn on imaginations. Politics ends up being a battle of imaginations, even of conspiracy theories. While moving politics to the less than fully rational, the public, or even the articulable terrain of the imagination is surely a huge problem for political systems that still imagine the world in Enlightened terms, a politics of the imagination affords considerable room for the intervention of the intellectual. Rephrased, if politics is all about how one views the world, then intellectuals, who spend time and energy working out their view of matters, have a chance to do politics. Refunctioned ethnography can support a truly public anthropology by articulating—and to at least that extent, rationalizing—the irrational (or post or prerational) that informs political imagination and so politics. So articulated, one might begin to think about how to respond, and to whom, in order to get something done. One might begin to think, that is, about how to intervene.

Thus the possibility of thoughtful politics, the Enlightenment dream of a government founded upon "reflection and choice," requires recognizing that, in most situations, familiar liberal notions of what makes politics— ideas like participation, representation, and rationality—are hardly relevant, for the simple reason that such notions give us little purchase over the social constellations that determine our politics. If we are willing to study how imaginations and power coalesce, however, we may find ourselves in a position to say something. In helping us to navigate our own politics, a politics that we understand is not transparent to us, refunctioned ethnography can serve as a way station between our Enlightened political commitments and our surreal lives.

*   *   *

Ethnography for present situations takes a stance toward politics quite different from the stance taken by classical, or indeed much contemporary, cultural anthropology. If the navigator wishes to be political in a serious sense—hardly a foregone conclusion—then the navigator must learn about the swirls and assemblages of this world, which cannot really be done from outside. If she wishes to reflect upon how politics is done, she must first participate, at least imaginatively. And if she wishes to intervene, especially without her own source of authority, she must do so in terms that appeal to those inside.

Such complicity can easily lead to feelings of guilt. Politics is ugly, not just in its mechanics and details, but due to the fact that order, by definition, suppresses things that, at least in some circumstances, one would hope to see liberated. And some politics, like wars, are mind-bendingly ugly. (Mauss is said to have lost his mind when confronted with another war.)

As this text is written, anthropologists are being asked to assist in the formulation of a security policy more attuned to its cultural circumstances, and therefore more effective. This is not new—much of area studies has a military upbringing—but it again presents the ethnographer as unavoidably complicit in the machinations of power. The intellectual's hands are not clean.

There are of course many things to say in response. Certainly intellectuals should participate in the defense of their societies. And the only thing worse than the cooption of the intellectual by power is power that ignores the intellectual's contribution altogether, as was convincingly demonstrated in the first years of the present war. But my point here is not that anthropologists should support this or that policy or should try to avoid political entanglements altogether. My point is far more simple: insofar as they wish to do politics, ethnographers will be involved, indeed complicit. And therefore guilty.

But even guilt should not be overdone, lest it become a form of moral aggrandizement. The ethnographer is no more responsible for the course of politics than navigators are responsible for the seas through which they sail.

CHAPTER EIGHTEEN

Ethnography and the Bureaucratic University

As a social matter, the university has never been healthier. The university is more central to the operation of this society than it has been to any society in which it has existed. A society founded on meritocratic capitalism that espouses democratic ideals needs institutions in which large numbers of people can be assigned to their places. For the foreseeable future, we may be assured that universities will continue to teach "business," "law," "creative writing," and "philosophy," and down the ladder a few rungs, "criminal justice" and "social work." The university, like bureaucracy more generally, is a well-nigh universal institutional technology. But the fact that a curriculum can be devised and students can be sorted hardly constitutes an argument that this is the best way to go about a given intellectual activity. Indeed, there is a substantial risk that the university thus conceived, our university, already has ceased to be respectable as a place for thought.

It has become widely argued (and I agree) that the modern ideal of the university, associated with Humboldt's University of Berlin, exported from Germany to the United States and thence to the rest of the world, has died. What we might, following Bill Readings, call the "university of culture" has been silently and almost completely replaced with an essentially bureaucratic concatenation, unified by the notion of "excellence." The causes of the university of culture's decline have been many. The fragmentation of knowledge, the fundamentally indefensible divisions among the disciplines, and the decline of authority of various claims to truth have all tended to make the university a less coherent environment. The great social pressures placed on universities in recent decades by their democratization (and the associated professionalization of vast stretches of economic and cultural life) have made the university of culture's often amateurish ideals for intellectual life ("the well-rounded student," the "love of learning") seem stunningly impractical. One could go on, but for now it suffices to say that the University, which had once seemed a great Idea, has come to seem incoherent and unrealistic. So the university as ideal has faded, and conversely, the vast grasslands of bureaucratic institutions have come to seem more significant.

Despite its social necessity, the bureaucratic university is hardly an overwhelming success. The bureaucratic university strikingly remains organized by statist institutions and forms, despite incessant calls for internationalization within the university and the realities of globalization without. Tests, standards, and aid are provided or overseen by states (or corporations acting in lieu of the state). The state licenses the professions through the university (one of Kant's points in *The Conflict of the Faculties*), and outright nationalism—the nation as organizational trope—is substantively evident in the social sciences and the humanities (national histories, literatures, ethnographies, economics), if less obvious in the natural sciences. If we look to how the natural sciences are done, however, we see that an inordinate amount of funding is provided by national governments or justified as in the national interest.

One could go on, but this is enough to suggest that the university, born in Prussia of all places, remains a profoundly nationalist institution. Perhaps this makes some sense, even today, in the United States, which is big and powerful enough to function in most ways as a nation in the old-fashioned sense. But if all the talk of globalization and great transformation and the like means anything, surely it must mean that the nation-state is no longer an adequately powerful conception to give us much purchase on the shape and dynamics of contemporary social life. In consequence, insofar as the university is tacitly structured by the nation-state, then the university is profoundly out of step with this time.

Even when university life is paid for not by nations but by corporations that are themselves large-scale bureaucracies, the contemporary university is deeply committed to bureaucracy, to a view of modern life as rational (or at least juridical), to Weber, to policy, and to the exercise of collective power through the state and other hierarchical institutions. But there are huge problems with rationalistic bureaucracy as a model of intellectual life, however, and hence with the place that the bureaucratic university has carved out for itself in contemporary global society. Bureaucracy is hardly a term of affection. Pedantry has always been a problem but never more so than now, when bureaucratic principles of jurisdiction (discipline) and procedure (method) are held up as the essence of intellectual life. But jurisdiction and procedure are officially offered as answers, substitutes for thought, rather than questions, opportunities to think. If it becomes obvious that little thinking is done in the academy, thinkers will tend to go elsewhere, and the intellectual honor due the institution will (and should) decline accordingly.

Moreover, while bureaucracy is undeniably an aspect of contemporary life, contemporary global politics is beneath rational. Indeed, the City of Gold is intentionally structured in ways that make Enlightened rationality expressed through a national context difficult if not impossible to achieve. The point of doing politics through markets is that the gut leads the head; we have constructed a politics of desire. (Rationality has been reconceived as the achievement of desire; this is the achievement of the economists.) In such a world, bureaucratic structures are always less interesting than the mediation and negotiation of desires. Rephrased, Weber's iron cage is hardly erotic; contemporary life is, and so is the advertising industry. But bureaucrats—and so professors—are not usually very sexy.

The postmodern critiques of the academy made in anthropology, law, and elsewhere in the '80s did not go nearly far enough. If the nation, and, in particular, the notion that the nation is the context for political participation through rational argument (republican democracy) have come to seem implausible (because markets and bureaucracies in different ways make what intellectuals do [read, think, argue] seem worthless) then the intellectual worthiness of the frame of the university is called into question. Why are thoughtful people, intellectuals in a simply positive sense, to treasure islands of merely bureaucratic rationality (that is, of a rationality that is widely despised as formal, narrow, and senseless) adrift in a sparkling but hardly rational ocean of global capitalism? Why not regard the public and private university as like either the postal service or Federal Express, institutions that no doubt confront problems that require considerable intelligence but who cares, apart from employees? (How much do employees care?) There are answers, of course. Indeed, those of us who teach have little choice but to give ourselves answers. My point is that the specifically intellectual honor due the bureaucratic university cannot be taken for granted. Is the university worth our allegiance, even devotion? Or is it just another job?

Let us take seriously the proposition that the university is not automatically worth our intellectual loyalties. If true, this would raise serious questions about the status of cultural anthropology (and so ethnography, however refunctioned) as an institutionalized academic subject. Chapter 15, "One Discipline among Others," sought to articulate how ethnography did its own work, produced knowledge even within the already known, that was not likely to be produced by other academic disciplines. But supposing that the bureaucratic university in fact does need ethnography, should we respect the activity so defined? Assuming that ethnography fills a role not performed by some other discipline in the bureaucratic university does not suffice to make ethnography worthy of respect. A competitive advantage within the academy, a successful specialization, is hardly enough to make ethnography more than crassly worthwhile. Although "ethnography through thick and thin" has a certain harmonic resonance to it, we might be disinclined to say "farm subsidies through thick and thin," or "zoning variances through thick and thin." A given bureaucracy may have a competitive advantage over loosely analogous enterprises, may even be socially necessary, without demanding intellectual attention, still less affection. If the university is not worthy of respect, then any utility ethnography may have to the institution does not serve as a specifically intellectual justification of the enterprise. Therefore, if we wish to justify the institutionalization of ethnography within the academy, some more affirmative defense of ethnography's work in the institution is required.

Let us begin by clarifying the proposition that the shift in character of the idea of the university from a university of culture (and back of that, a university of Truth) to a bureaucratic university, has been accompanied by a diminution in respect for the institution. The situation is complex, of course—many academics cannot imagine doing anything else—but contemporary disappointment with the university may be anatomized along the following familiar lines:

1. The contemporary university is fragmented, even balkanized.
2. The contemporary university is isolated, even parochial. Academics speak to other academics, with little attention to the excitements of other ways of life.
3. The contemporary university is boring, essentially just another large bureaucratic institution, and no more intrinsically interesting than others.

Ethnography for present situations addresses each of these discontents. First, the university is indeed fragmented, but fragmentation is also the contemporary condition. In the course of its history, the university has been held together by Christendom, the state, and then, for a while, an increasingly secularized and amorphous idea of liberal culture (including the sciences), but such coherences no longer work, in our experience of the world or its simulacrum, the university. In its very fragmentation, then, the university has at least been true to its time. But it is precisely this condition of fragmentation that makes multisited ethnography so necessary—the navigator's task, orientation among points of different distance and significance, is true whether we consider "the real world" or that map known as the university. Ethnography for present situations can be useful to the modern university for the same reason and in the same way that it can be useful for approaching the world: ethnography brings things that had been disparate into relation with one another.

Similarly, in setting out into the world and reporting back to the university, the navigator works against the cultural isolation, even parochialism, that threatens all established bureaucracies, including the contemporary university, as a condition of their specialization, stability, and authority. Surely the anxieties of the invisible college of discontented academics—that they are isolated, that other things are happening elsewhere, that they have chosen the wrong career and marooned themselves—have some truth. Other things are indeed happening elsewhere; the university is hardly the only site of knowledge production. But there is no need to feel marooned. One might ask other people what they are doing. One might travel. Ethnography for present situations is constructed precisely for such ventures.

Even the bureaucratic university is not literally boring—almost all the world is mirrored, in some fashion, within the academy. "Boredom" is a euphemism for something darker, a sense of intellectual alienation from the (fragmented and isolated) professional discourses that comprise so much of academic life. So many academics are emotionally disengaged. What started out as the pursuit of truth became something far more modest, not all that interesting, and therefore called "boring." This is quite sad, common, and generally unnecessary. What ethnography for present situations has to teach the university writ large is nothing less than why and how to have a thoughtful but unprofessional conversation.

But the bureaucratic university offers something to ethnographers, too. Navigators need harbors. The university affords the opportunity, still, of leisure, reflection, and time to talk. The university buys time for ethnographers to cultivate a sophisticated understanding of what this moment, this stage of events, feels like in this place, when a particular constellation of phenomena seems important. And that sensitivity is something worth having, especially these days. Indeed it is perhaps this sense of languorous pregnancy that is most precious, in a world where slowness is so rare, about ethnography for present situations.

CHAPTER NINETEEN

From Science to Romance

Perhaps the funniest aspect of classical cultural anthropology has been its pretensions to scientific objectivity, despite massive evidence of a variety of all too human interests. What red-blooded young man in cold gray London after the carnage of World War One would not want to know as much as possible about the sexual habits of the Trobriand Islanders? By the time Rabinow's highly modernist reflections on his essentially traditional fieldwork, including an account—*très moderne, certainement*—of missing Paris '68 but getting laid in Morocco, had become a classic, the discipline had made some peace with the temptations at its core. There are reasons to speak of sexual knowledge; there is truth in the awareness of what we now capitalize as the Other; the lines of innocence, repression, and shame are much of who we are. Cultural anthropology has always been about these rather biblical matters.

Less salaciously, and now that an important arc of the history of cultural anthropology is evident if not quite complete, it is not too difficult to trace a line from Rousseau and the romantic discovery of Nature generally through the Orientalist tradition in nineteenth-century art, and especially the romance and travel literature that occupied so much of the late nineteenth- and early twentieth-century mind in the countries where anthropology was founded. Nor was anthropology the only science to be conducted through romantic obsessions for which it had no adequate language. Consider the glorious pretensions of mountain climbers and other explorers, sometimes dying with rocks in their pockets. Perhaps more strangely still, and to this day, even the most physical sciences, and the most exuberant materialists, cultivate the ideal of the genius.

One might think that ethnography for present situations would turn away from all this romantic nonsense, which has such a Victorian (and juvenile) ring. Yet ethnography for present situations has its own *frisson*, its own sense of uncovering. Much of this is biographical. Cultural anthropology still sends idealistic people in their sexually charged twenties out "into the field," that is, out of the zones of their usual connections, constraints, and responsibilities, often far from home. There is still an important sense in which this is the academic institutionalization of travel literature, and more deeply, of rites of passage: young people are told to chart a journey and return with something worth knowing ... Sexual habits have changed somewhat, and many of the young people are female, but nonetheless surely this sounds in very old registers of much more than anthropology? But even in its postmodern key, there is something brave and exciting and more than a little sexy about young people setting out.

If we borrow the gendered language of another age, the ethnography for present situations urged in this book seems decidedly more feminine than the classical imagination of ethnography. The navigator must inspire others to act on her behalf. She must find liaisons, make connections, network in order to reach important subjects (the navigator is likely to be something of a courtesan). She must make her project appealing to her subjects, who are frankly considered to be active participants (collaborators or interlocutors) in the enterprise rather than the objects of a young man's analysis, as in the classical imagination. Without the ability to rely on scientific or cultural (colonial) authority, ethnography for present situations must become attractive, perhaps even seductive.

While it is easy enough and kind of fun to understand any number of human activities erotically, not all such activities can properly be called romantic. The erotics of ethnography for present situations is indeed romantic, however, in its insistence on the importance of subjective human connections (and hence the emotional, the irrational, the aesthetic) over against a world that is perceived to be, or be socially discussed as, overly deterministic, rationalistic, and ultimately inhuman. One cannot imagine romanticism in literature (or culture generally) without Enlightenment; one cannot imagine ethnography for present situations without profound misgivings about what is vaguely called modernization (or these days, globalization). The romantic impulse clearly infuses, indeed sustains, cultural anthropology at the present time, even among those who are hardly refunctioning ethnography. The insistence on outsider status, the automatic valorization of designated victims, and even the calling for a public anthropology in practice reflect prior adoption of a rather romantic political stance from which anthropological work begins.

This is not to say that political romanticism is found only among cultural anthropologists. One sees much the same thing across legal scholarship, where progressives say similar things, and even many conservatives, in their impatience with the constraints of living in contemporary society (regulations and such), display pronounced Arcadian tendencies. More generally, romanticism arises from across the political landscape as a common critical response to certain situations. Romantics thus tends to be inconsistent—but this may be less a sign of their intellectual weakness than evidence that very different people assess their situations in roughly similar, but hardly identical, ways. So, confronted with Weber's iron cage, or the City of Gold, or however one wishes to articulate the current situation, any number of very different people have what broadly speaking could be called romantic responses. What else is left?

If we restrict the inquiry to cultural anthropology for a moment, and if romanticism is in fact prevalent in cultural anthropology today, then the efforts to purge anthropology of its romanticism (under the heading of exoticism, one step away from pernicious Orientalism), made in the '80s and since, have not been wholly successful. The demons that anthropology as "cultural studies" thought it had exorcised return at the heart of ethnography for present situations, if perhaps in more feminine guise. Perhaps a degree of the romantic (even the exotic!) is intrinsic to the ethnographic encounter, even as reconfigured. To understand the space of a culture, or a present situation, the strange context must become familiar. Inhabitants must become people. Even while familiarization is pursued in order to construct an objective description, a structural map, to familiarize is also to bring into relationship with oneself, and thus inevitably one's body, at least by visiting. But such encounters can be more or less intense and more or less benign. Conquests and surrenders of various sorts beckon. The sexually intimate is the familiarization par excellence . . . The venture, the setting out and learning, has an erotic structure.

But this erotic structure is neither enough for romanticism, nor is it all that is entailed in doing ethnography today. Ethnography for present situations attempts to find meaning in a world that has too many mechanisms for stripping meaning out of social relations, that is, bureaucratization, technological displacement, social alienation, globalization, and so forth. Because ethnography for present situations takes place vis-à-vis modernity, and because the modern is at least superficially understood as both rational and meaningless, refunctioned ethnography will tend to valorize the irrational, the passion beneath the surface, in an effort to discern (or even insist upon) human meaning. And it is this conflict that is truly romantic, and so necessary, despite all the problems.

Yet the persistence of romantic responses should give one pause. Caution is in order. Romance can be foolish, immoral, even dangerous. Much of the romanticism implicit in classical ethnography has been rightly criticized as persiflage for the colonial and objectivizing tendencies entailed in ethnographic practice. To consider something exotic is to go a considerable distance towards dehumanizing it; much "Orientalism" looks racist (even if the race card is played early and too often). Moreover, even at its best, romanticism is inherently a rather sentimental stance. A realist, to say nothing of rigorous, appreciation of other lives, values, and even cultures should perhaps begin by emptying itself, to the extent possible, of its own sentimental preconceptions, prejudices really, about the people who one is interested in learning from . . . and so forth.

Nor should we be too sanguine about the fact that contemporary romanticism is so much more politically correct than that bad old Orientalism. Romanticism in politics always begins by talking about freedom, but all too often ends in blood—consider a short lesson in modern history, beginning with Burke's *Reflections on the Revolution in France* and working through Conrad's *Heart of Darkness* to any number of present wars or indeed, failures to impose order through violence. This is not the place for an excursion into contemporary politics, but it is worth remembering how much talk of freedom surrounds the current war. This is true of most U.S. wars, but this is not specifically American—all Africa speaks of freedom. Perhaps some such freedom will be achieved in the course of time, but recent experience demonstrates that contemporary sentiments (which we may or may not characterize as romantic rebellions against an unfeeling modernity) can and are being deployed for deeply unfortunate ends. This is not the best of all possible worlds, and our romantic tendencies are in part to blame (but so are our rationalist tendencies—there are reasons for rebellion!).

Less dramatically, many aspects of the anthropological enterprise simply do not lend themselves to romanticization, at least not at first blush. The academic setting of, many of the patrons for, and many of the topics investigated by contemporary anthropology are deeply bureaucratic. Much of modern life is collaborative, interconnected, official, rational, boring—and contemporary ethnography must reflect and express that, too. For all the allure of romanticism, the methodological, institutional, and social difficulties presented by romanticism as an intellectual modus operandi cannot be ignored. Nor, as suggested above, is romanticism a completely attractive or even sufficient political (and hence moral and in that sense intellectual) stance. These general objections are lent special force by a contemporary social fact that must be confronted: students today are not particularly romantic. In comparison with living memory, this is an unromantic age. Earnestness (bespeaking the capacity and willingness to compete) pervades our best universities; disengagement (bespeaking the opposite) suffuses the lower reaches of the educational system. The romanticism that does exist is largely expressed through strikingly naïve forms of political posturing in which the posturing overwhelms the political.

And yet one must not confuse symptom with underlying cause. The university, including anthropology, may be unromantic or just boring, in fact, but that may be because ways to be exciting have not been found. Much of this book has been an effort to conceive and articulate an attractive dramatic setting, a winsome poetics, not just for an ethnography designed to explore present situations but, at least suggestively, for an engaged intellectual life. Obviously, there are alternatives, some of them very dour—many of us are indeed living such dour alternatives. But unhappiness, professional or otherwise, does not mean that romance is not possible. The lonely should not remain silent and brood upon the impossibility of contact but should instead start conversations. The romantic—properly understood, hardly pith helmets and heading upriver stuff—aspects of refunctioned ethnography or, much more generally, the persistence of what might broadly be called romantic responses to present situations, should be emphasized rather than denied. The classical ethnographer fled outside modernity and used the vantage point of the foreign culture to gain purchase on modernity—the critical edge that anthropology has always displayed. The navigator attempts to understand how variously situated humans, in contemporary circumstances, construct worlds that allow them to function (as they obviously do), and what their practices might mean for the rest of us. In doing so, she articulates a much more humanized understanding of a hitherto facelessly mechanistic, or just inchoate or even altogether unknown, aspect of our contemporaneity. So if, and with caution, the romantic character of this enterprise is embraced, what follows?

Let me offer three complimentary ways of seeing this problem. The first, already mentioned, is psychological. The second is more epistemological, and the third, which I will only suggest, is ontological. First, psychologically, a traditional way to understand Romanticism (Goethe) is as a way of finding a place for passion within the intellectual frame of the Enlightenment. Thus Goethe can be understood not merely as a rebellion against the rationalistic classicism of Enlightened aesthetics but also as a psychological deepening and thus humanizing of the Enlightenment. The matter is of course complicated—Goethe would also go on to develop his own classicism and denounce romanticism of a certain sort. For present purposes, however, the Enlightenment began (or was ideologically articulated as) a commonsense rationalism, which required a turn to psychology and the insistence that psychology was inevitably part of the human condition and, more problematically still, the apparatus of knowledge. Kant's philosophy would do this in stunningly dry and rationalistic language, but Schiller the poet was one of the best readers of Kant. Romanticism has thus always been about what cultural anthropologists since the '80s have called reflexivity, and so here again we see the affinity between the anthropological impulse and what in art and culture generally is called romanticism.

All of this plays out in somewhat smaller compass within the academy. The rupture of the '80s was a romantic rebellion against a dry academic rationality that drew strength from the ultimately undeniable lack of self-consciousness (at least published self-consciousness) of the preceding generation. And here, again, familiar discomforts with romantic enthusiasms arise. We must ask to what extent should academics publish their self-consciousness? Is the academy not already therapeutic enough? Confession is a difficult performance to bring off gracefully, and classicism has much to recommend it as a stance. This raises very old questions of academic (and artistic) aesthetics, the tension between romantic and classical, between Dionysus and Apollo, and so forth, none of which need be answered here. For now it suffices to note that the classicism that might emerge after such a rebellion, however, is hardly superficial rationalism but is instead a conscious acknowledgment (and suppression, at least in public) of romantic yearnings at the heart of the enterprise.

Second, epistemologically, anthropology should be happy to acknowledge the romantic aspects of its enterprise because intellectuals are deeply in need of romance. Romanticism is not just psychologically necessary for freshening up the iron cage of modernity but has become conceptually needful. As discussed in various ways throughout this book, the creation of connections, modes of understanding, are required for doing business and otherwise living today. Ways of thinking must be created now, because the conceptual categories we long understood as "modern," most obviously, the political conceptions derived from the nation-state, are no longer serviceable for many purposes. Once the conceptual categories become less trenchant, then ordinary rationality, and in particular, statistical modes of analysis based upon such categories, lose much of their purchase. So, for example, the idea of a gross domestic product (GDP) assumes that we know what the bounds of the national economy are and what constitutes a product. In a largely service and intellectual economy operating through foreign direct investment and a supranational capital market, these questions are, to be diplomatic, not trivial. My iPod was "designed in California" and "assembled in China." Indeed. What are the categories that matter?

"What matters" is something about which romantic intuition, sometimes in rebellion, often has quite a lot to say. People do make sense of contemporary business, or life more generally, after a fashion. People tell themselves and each other stories, often using vocabulary (such as GDP, or money supply) that is understood to be mysteriously imprecise. The numbers are still there, but they are somewhat floating, surreal, tethered by rumors. Such cultural poetry, mythmaking, against a backdrop of rationalism felt to be impoverished, is undeniably romantic.

It might be argued that cultural knowledge always has consisted of stories, and so this time is no different from any other. This might even be true. But, at least ideologically, modernity sought to banish this sort of knowledge. Cultural knowledge was what traditional cultures had, and what would be lost when they were folded into modern rational societies, leaving only their traces in university libraries. For our part, we moderns could talk about the "nation" and the "economy" and the "law"—the list goes on—without hesitation. This is clearly no longer our intellectual situation. At present, such modernist talk is objectively possible (listen to any political speech) but tends to sound very stilted. Contemporary intellectuals demand new articulations that allow thought and even more vitally, conversation, to proceed. The hope here is that the reconfiguration of ethnography, as well as its attendant romanticism, can help to foster understandings that we need no longer call by the derivative name of postmodern. We might even be able to look back and see that period we vaguely identify as modern and understand it in the limited but clear fashion of descendants, as now we may speak of medieval Paris or Periclean Athens.

While we might begin talking about the romantic character of ethnography for present situations as a rebellion against the constraints of globalized modernity (what I have called the psychological), as with comedy or sex, the real significance is not in the rebellion but in the seeing anew (the epistemological, and even the ontological). In social thought and elsewhere, romance is load bearing. In this time, in which the social generally and intellectual life more particularly remain overly dependent on dubious categories, the opportunity for ethnography is to follow the best of its romantic inclinations to generate new combinations, new articulations, and new forms for thought. Doing this well—writing well—will of course require a degree of discipline, a certain stiffness, tendencies that aesthetically are directly expressed as classicism.

Does the village dance lead to bed and then children? Let me rephrase: does the psychological necessity and epistemological gain of the romanticism that we discover within the grain of ethnography as we have thought through its refunctioning suggest similar things about our responses to the contemporary world through which navigators move? Certainly. And it would also seem that our rethinking of the world, a world that is after all so very constructed, would be likely to have material consequences, consequences that would work to constrain and enable new possibilities. Thus "romance" is importantly, but not only, a psychological requirement in a cold world. Nor is romance merely a gesture toward the possibility of re-combining and shifting categories, a gain for thought and for the processes of our thinking, epistemology. Romance is not only the mark of curiosity about the world as it emerges from the recombinations studied by the navigator, it has an ontological significance: romance is the promise of the world engendered by the exercise of curiosity, of play, and of discovery, for which the ancient metaphor (and much more than a metaphor) is sexual knowledge, after which the world is different for all concerned. Romance signals the presence of a vessel within the vessel of ethnography, potential that is always near and never yet known. It is this potential, just beyond thought, desire, and fortune, that this book has proposed to greet cheerfully.

It is this cheerfulness that I have set against the aesthetic of so much contemporary thought. This is not to deny that thought may well be sad; everything goes downward in Plato. But it bears remembering that from time to time, Plato arises, and is hardly born of thought. Philosophy is less than life. And far more often, there is occasion to talk. So yes, bed and then children. Our ability to think through such matters is very limited, rather more in the nature of dreaming, or speculations that we tell ourselves are rational. For present purposes, the idea of romance is a winsome reminder of the human capacity to make the world anew, the knowledge that we will, too, and the hope that we acquit ourselves well. But it is often good to nurture hopes in silence, and this is enough.

*   *   *

If I were to criticize this book, I would argue that it overestimates the ability of most professional knowledge workers, its readers, to let go and be amateurs, and so intellectual in that sense, without the authority of their institutions to back them. Anyone who has spent much time in a university will witness a huge amount of insecurity, often expressed rather aggressively and almost always unfortunate. In the face of that reality, this book insouciantly argues that people should play the fool, maybe wise but often not, and just start conversations with people. This book argues that not only is intellectual life not impossible, in some very important ways, it is not even very difficult. But after going through the wringer required to become a full-time academic, few people have the confidence or the energy for such play. This is sad.

But so what? Conversations do happen. And any account of ethnography that begins from an actual conversation, and that takes the possibility of conversation as its premise, and that hopes something new will emerge out of such encounters, is not in a position to deny its playful, even romantic, commitments. Here again, more deeply than could be discussed above, ethnography differs from its inverse, journalism. Where journalism reports, analyzes, critiques (all of which require distance), ethnography learns, understands, combines—all of which require participation, working together, over time. And who knows what will emerge from such romantic encounters? That attitude is what makes ethnography for present situations, and could make intellectual life more generally, unpredictable, exciting, and deeply meaningful going forward.

CHAPTER TWENTY

Reprise

Let me finish by asking an embarrassingly simple-minded question: What is ethnography for? This is an outsider's question. Professional anthropologists, like my friends George and Doug, tend to assume the discipline that authorizes them. For an academic anthropologist, why ethnography? is fairly idle, a parlor game, unless the termination of an academic program is being seriously contemplated, at which point the game might become existential. Assuming the discipline in broad outline, including ethnography, however, one might nonetheless ask, what are today's questions? How should adepts face these intellectual challenges and opportunities? Such questions, which Doug and George have been (re)asking for many years, frame part 1 of this book, although I try to suggest why the answers might matter outside anthropology.

Part 2 attempts to address these questions in fairly general fashion by sketching an integrated way for anthropologists to refunction, that is, both transform and preserve, ethnography in order to explore present situations.

Part 3 is informed by essentially institutional questions. What does this ethnography for present situations mean within the academic traditions of cultural anthropology in the United States (chapter 11)? Is cultural anthropology, understood in terms of such an open idea of ethnography, sufficiently coherent and rigorous to be institutionalized as a constitutive part, perhaps the center of gravity, of an academic discipline? (chapters 12–14). What niche would such cultural anthropology occupy in the academic ecosystem? Or, to use economic language, is cultural anthropology so understood sufficiently specialized to be considered a job? Unsurprisingly, part 3 answers all these questions affirmatively: ethnography for present situations can work in the setting of the university. But the conclusion is somewhat foregone, because academic cultural anthropology was assumed from the beginning.

This part 4 shifts perspectives and asks, what is cultural anthropology—even based upon a substantial reconceptualization of ethnography—for? from the viewpoint of an outsider, a student perhaps, or someone like me, a member of another faculty, who has no stake in the profession of anthropology. Once upon a time, the question was so easy it would not have been asked. In a world of obscure islands, simply learning what was on the islands was enough. And if the encounter with the exotic made us reconsider the familiar, if we learned about Paris while we were in Tahiti, so much the better. And not so long ago, cultural anthropology had a broad audience among intellectuals who were not themselves anthropologists. Many people, both outside and inside anthropology, have had great difficulty giving up this classical imagination of the field, even though the uncharted spaces on the map are long gone and the subjects and concerns of research have changed.

Despite the obvious differences, however, the contemporary situation is perhaps more similar to that lost world than we realize. Each of us thinks we know—well, somebody else knows—what makes this or that scene function. Thus, for each of us, most knowledge is elsewhere, that is to say, we do not really know. We mistake assumption for knowledge. Markets must be efficient; drugs must be safe; wars must be fought . . . and so forth. Our world of ostensibly perfect information is in fact perfect information about superficialities. Refunctioned ethnography presents a way for us to get to know our own worlds. The unsettling part of the enterprise is our realization that we have deluded ourselves into thinking we already understood.

Part 4 of this book has situated refunctioned ethnography vis-à-vis the vagaries of politics, a critique of the university, and hence the social situation of the academic, who must find new ways to an intellectual. Needless to say, these issues are not the exclusive concern of anthropologists. But—as these last chapters have tried to show—refunctioned ethnography has a great deal to contribute to our understanding of our situations. Refunctioned ethnography has much to say about how particular forms of politics are done in the context of globalization; about how the bureaucratic university may engage with the world; and indeed about how academics may engage with each other. Perhaps most surprising of all, the practice of ethnography has much to teach about how to be happy as an intellectual. Thus it is in response to the current disorientation among intellectuals generally, not merely the unresolved quandaries within the academic discipline of cultural anthropology, that a refunctioned ethnography might begin anew, to start conversations with other people, who move through different spaces in our shared world, perhaps worth our attention.